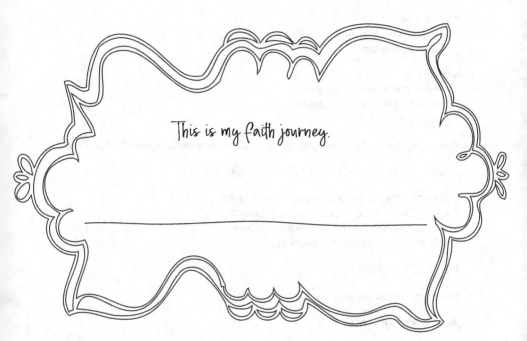

This is my faith journey.

Nihil obstat:
  Msgr. Michael Heintz,
  Censor librorum

Imprimatur:
  †Most Rev. Kevin C. Rhoades,
  Bishop of Fort Wayne–South Bend
  September 24, 2019

Cover, interior design and composition by Laurie Nelson, Agápe Design Studios.

Graphic elements: © iStockphoto.com, © Adobe Stock

ISBN 978-1-68192-531-8 (Inventory No. T2420)
1. RELIGION—Christian Life—Spiritual growth.
2. RELIGION—Christian Life—Woman's Issues.
3. RELIGION—Christianity—Catholic.

LCCN: 2020932278

PRINTED IN THE UNITED STATES OF AMERICA

Acknowledgments

Scripture quotations marked (NIV) are taken from the *Holy Bible, New International Version*®, NIV®. Copyright © 1973, 1978, 1984, 2011 by Biblica, Inc.™ Used by permission of Zondervan. All rights reserved worldwide. www.zondervan.com. The "NIV" and "New International Version" are trademarks registered in the United States Patent and Trademark Office by Biblica, Inc.™

Scripture quotations marked (NLT) are taken from the *Holy Bible, New Living Translation*, copyright ©1996, 2004, 2015 by Tyndale House Foundation. Used by permission of Tyndale House Publishers, a Division of Tyndale House Ministries, Carol Stream, Illinois 60188. All rights reserved.

Scripture quotations marked (NRSVCE) are from the *New Revised Standard Version Bible: Catholic Edition*, copyright © 1989, 1993 National Council of the Churches of Christ in the United States of America. Used by permission. All rights reserved worldwide.

Quotes from the *Catechism of the Catholic Church* are taken from the English translation of the Catechism of the Catholic Church for the United States of America, 2nd ed. Copyright 1997 by United States Catholic Conference—Libreria Editrice Vaticana.

Journals for Catholic Women

Seeking Peace

A Spiritual Journey from Worry to Trust

Allison Gingras

Dedication:

Writing is not glamorous; it requires a lot of sacrifice, especially by those who must live with the writer. Thank you to the following people for their continued support and many sacrifices:

Deacon Hubby Kevin and our amazing kids, Ian, Adam, and Faith; and

My beloved, incredible spiritual director, Deacon Gerald Ryan, and my courageous, heart-of-gold Dad, John Perry — may they both rest in the peace of Christ.

I have great gratitude for my #SaintPosse, who always has my back:

Saint Thérèse, (my friend) Saint Faustina, Venerable Patrick Peyton, Blessed Solanus Casey, Blessed Stanley Rother, my (hardworking) guardian angel, and Our Lady of Guadalupe.

Table of Contents

Introduction

Trust God if You Are Going to Trust God

"If you are going to trust God, then trust God." These wise words were often spoken to me by my beloved spiritual director, Deacon Gerald (Jerry) Ryan, who passed away in January of 2019. Deacon Jerry thoughtfully guided my faith journey for more than ten years. His style was direct yet always kind, especially when providing direction in my constant battle to trust God.

My lifelong struggle with anxiety complicates my ability to trust. Trusting the people around me has never come easy; throw into the mix that faith is based primarily on the unseen, and the struggle gets even more real. In addition to my trust issues, I am also a world-class worrier. Worst-case scenarios are my specialty. While I realize my fears rarely rely on fact or even logic, I still tend to assume that every situation will come to a horrible, tragic conclusion. Deacon Jerry patiently talked me through many panic attacks, continually restoring my peace by drawing my attention back to Christ. He would remind me of the multitude of promises God has made to us in the Scriptures. He'd even point out places in my life where God was clearly present.

One example from Scripture really speaks to my heart — the exchange between Jesus and Peter following Peter's unproductive night of fishing:

> After he had finished speaking, [Jesus] said to Simon, "Put out into deep water and lower your nets for a catch." Simon said in reply, "Master, we have worked hard all night and have caught nothing, but at your command I will lower the nets." When they had done this, they caught a great number of fish and their nets were tearing." (Luke 5:4-6)

Peter, seemingly skeptical of the Lord's plan, still submitted to it and obeyed Jesus' instructions. Like Peter, I, also, am sometimes skeptical of the Lord's plans but will (eventually) comply and trust God — even if it takes a moment of desperation to get me there. I owe Deacon Jerry a debt of gratitude. Before he came into my life, whenever plans went awry or I felt God had abandoned me or perhaps didn't even exist, I would stop trusting God. Deacon Jerry taught me that to stay steadfast in the faith, I had to believe in what I say I believe in.

You see a pattern with this dear man's thought process: if you are going to have faith, have faith; if you are going to believe, then believe; if you are going to trust, then trust.

Over the last ten years, my consent to the Lord's plans has increased exponentially, even when I've felt overwhelmed by clouds of doubt or fear. Before I began giving more time to prayer, participating in the sacraments, and reading Scripture — what I lovingly refer to as the "grace trifecta" (my own term) — I hardly ever surrendered my anxiety to the Lord. Not every obedient act results in the abundant harvest Peter enjoyed, or the one I may have hoped for or expected when I surrendered. The real reward comes in the strengthening of my faith and trust in Jesus and in building unwavering confidence that I will meet him one day in heaven.

Numerous are the miraculous, remarkable ways the Lord has blessed my cooperation with the nudges of the Holy Spirit! To this day, I can hear Deacon Jerry's joyful, compassionate, yet resolute voice in my head: "If you are going to trust God, kiddo, then you have no other choice but to trust God."

My anxieties stem mainly from my fear of the unknown, but, when I was growing up, my faulty perceptions of God exacerbated these anxieties. I grew up thinking God was waiting for me to mess up so he could "smote" me. There were only two outcomes to life: if you behaved well, you would go to heaven; if you didn't, you would be sent to "h-e-double-hockey-sticks." There was no talk at home about God as gentle and caring, no discussions about Jesus as Savior, no conversations about Mary as our interceding, protective mother. Moments to share our faith were infrequent, and the ones I can recall usually involved me feeling uncomfortable, petrified, or bored.

No Anxiety at All

The title of this **Stay Connected Journal** comes from the first Bible verse I ever memorized, Philippians 4:4–7. The minute I read it, I knew these words needed to be committed to memory:

> Rejoice in the Lord always. I shall say it again: rejoice! Your kindness should be known to all. The Lord is near. Have no anxiety at all, but in everything, by prayer and petition, with thanksgiving, make your requests known to God. Then the peace of God that surpasses all understanding will guard your hearts and minds in Christ Jesus.

As a woman with lifelong, chronic anxiety, hearing these words was life-changing. In them, Saint Paul lays out a roadmap for approaching the circumstances of our lives that stir anxiety within us.

He begins by telling us to rejoice in the Lord, always — that is, to find joy in what the Lord is doing in our lives, in all circumstances and in all ways. Life in the Spirit should be joyful!

Next, he reminds us to pray, to share our worries, cares, and concerns with the Lord. I love that we have a God who is not unaware of our need to ask, seek, and knock. What a gift it is that we can pray and ask for what we need! Prayer is a positive response to every situation, especially those beyond our control. So, bring your petitions to the Lord, remembering that he is near.

Then we have the most compelling part of this passage (and probably the most difficult to follow): "Have no anxiety ... ." Saint Paul reveals the secret to achieving less worry and more trust when he adds, "but in everything, by prayer and petition, with thanksgiving, make your requests known to God." Saint Paul reminds us not only to pray but also to be thankful to God in all things — in good times and bad, in sickness and health, in poverty and plenty. We are called to rejoice and to be faithful regardless of our circumstances.

Finally, Saint Paul brings it all home with words in which every worrier can find hope. Paul explains that when we practice joy and gratitude (regardless of our circumstances) and trustingly come to God with our petitions, our hearts and minds will be filled with "the peace of God that surpasses all understanding."

A Word of Caution

I have one word of caution before you embark on your journey with this **Stay Connected Journal**. This book deals with life's general worries and anxieties from a faith perspective; it is does not address the psychological and medical roots of chronic anxiety or depression. If you experience chronic anxiety, seek medical help; I promise you will not regret doing so. Over the years, my own treatment for anxiety has included medication and counseling. People sometimes wrongly believe that seeking professional help for anxiety is somehow failing to trust in God. Nothing could be farther from the truth.[1]

Furthermore, although this book outlines a spiritual approach to worry, please do not become discouraged if you find yourself unable to pray your way to peace. Learning to trust is a process; there is good reason Saint Paul often speaks of the need for perseverance in our faith journey.

My prayer for you is that this book helps you to recognize the places where anxiety arises in your life so that you can begin to bring those moments to Christ — and, in the end, find the deep peace that only he can give.

1: Building Trust through Life Experience

SEEKING PEACE: A SPIRITUAL JOURNEY

Opening Prayer

Almighty and ever-living God, guide me through this study as I learn how to trust you and accept your desire for me to have no anxiety at all. O Lord, may my heart and mind be filled with your strength, hope, and peace. Teach me to rely on your ever-present help not only in the more pressing concerns of my day but also in the everyday, ordinary moments of my life. In my daily comings and goings, I forget to include you in the journey. Lord, protect my heart from being burdened by the dread of what could be. Remind me of the truth of your love and your promise to always come to my assistance.

Father, all the memories of the past cause me great fear, worry, and anxiety. Heavenly Father, we know that you have sent your only Son, Our Lord Jesus Christ, to bring us peace — a peace, Saint Paul tells us, that surpasses all understanding. Lord, I too often fail to accept your gracious gift of peace. In doing so, I have lost sight of the mighty power and goodness behind your plan for my life — a plan for my good and not my woe, as the prophet Jeremiah says.

Help me begin to understand the root of my lack of trust. Help me to understand how prayer, the sacraments, and reading your Word provide me with the perfect blueprint for trusting in you. Dear Heavenly Father, thank you for adopting me into your family. May I recognize the beauty of being called your daughter, and how your eternal love overshadows me, protecting and soothing my troubled heart. Amen.

On My Heart

_____

_____

_____

_____

_____

_____

_____

_____

Daily Concerns

Jesus complained to me in these words: Distrust on the part of souls is tearing at My insides. The distrust of a chosen soul causes Me even greater pain; despite My inexhaustible love for them they do not trust Me. Even My death is not enough for them. Woe to the soul that abuses these [gifts].[2]

Woe to that soul, as that soul is mine! Despite all the blessings the Lord has bestowed on me and my family, my heart is often filled with an uneasy uncertainty. If it is any consolation,

Jesus, it's not just you whom I don't trust; I am kind of unsure of many things. My ability to trust needs bolstering via grace and focusing on my relationship with Jesus.

How I Became an Olympic Worrier

I may not be skilled in many things, but I have mastered worrying. My penchant for taking everyday occurrences and transforming them into monumental opportunities to worry is partly hereditary and partly learned. Long ago, I had to stop watching dramas on television and reading women's magazines. Every story spun my anxiety to dizzying heights with new possibilities for all the bad things that could happen in my life or to my loved ones. Every new cancer story had me looking for lumps and spots. Every fatal car accident made getting in a car petrifying. Every natural disaster made me question the safety of where I lived or where I would travel.

A super encouraging way to start a book on how to worry less, huh? Yet this is a vital step in moving forward: we must first look back. It is often in the past that we find the answers for a more peaceful future. Memories, even the most painful ones, are a beautiful gift.

History in the Making

I come from a long line of worrywarts. My maternal grandmother, with whom I spent many weekends as a child, worried about everything. My mother, terrified of thunderstorms, would huddle with us on the couch during every storm to pray the Rosary. Mind you, this was the only time my family prayed together. Then lightning struck our house, and that's all the proof we needed to convince us that prayer doesn't work. We never prayed together again.

We were not a family who had healthy, open discussions about our feelings or fears; nor were we a family that turned to our faith in times of difficulty (of which we had a great deal). I have vague childhood memories of attending church, especially with my paternal grand-mother ... but most of what I remember is the horrible singing and being hungry.

Where It All Began

While preparing to write this book, I spent some time in adoration before the Blessed Sacrament looking back at my life. I realized that my anxiety seemed to be rooted in a string of horrific experiences when I was about ten years old: the abduction and murder of a fif-teen-year-old girl from our town, our house being struck by light-ning (which I witnessed from a car in the driveway), and my dad's first major heart attack.

For nearly forty years, it was my father's continual brushes with death that fed my anxiety more than anything else. My father "died" while waiting to be seen in the hospital emergency department, prompt-ing my normally soft-spoken mother to run into the hall yelling, "He's dead! *Now* will someone help him?" The hospital was able to resusci-tate him, but our lives were never the same. Although it may have ap-peared that the only change in our home was the removal of salt from the table, the fear of losing my father — or any loved one — consumed me. My thoughts were constantly filled with worry about all things related to health. My personal health concerns reached new heights thanks to a not-so-helpful nurse who explained to my brother and me that my father's heart condition was hereditary, and we needed to start taking care of ourselves now or end up like him.

My understanding of the world as a scary, uncertain place was reinforced by many other events in my life growing up, for example, the unexpected death of my brother's teenage friend, murdered by her sister, and my parents' divorce. Lacking a stable family life, a faith community, and a relationship with God left me feeling abandoned, sad, and unsure. I developed acute anxiety, along with stomach pains that my doctor warned could turn into an ulcer. Yup, I have been training for the Worry Olympics for a very long time.

Waiting for the Other Shoe to Drop

My way of thinking and interacting with the world around me held zero peace. Instead, I always found myself waiting for the other shoe to drop, and it robbed me of my joy. While some might ask, "Why me?" when bad things happen to them, I would think of all that *could* happen and ask, "Why couldn't it be me?"

Looking back on my life, I see a strange pattern. Weeks after being hit by a drunk driver during my senior year of high school, I drove along the same road thinking I would probably never live long enough to graduate from high school. After I did, I immediately began thinking I would probably never live long enough to finish college. When I had accomplished that, I had the same thoughts of impending doom about getting married, having children, and owning a home ... and then, well, I did those things too. I was so busy worrying about missing out on life that I couldn't see these major life milestones as evidence of a blessed or fulfilled life.

This is not how God wants us to live. He has called us to live in peace: "Peace I leave with you; my peace I give to you. Not as the world gives do I give it to you. Do not let your hearts be troubled or afraid" (John 14:27). While I have experienced many difficulties and trials in my life, the Holy Spirit continually teaches me to recognize the circumstances which are not, and most likely never will be, my crosses to bear. My life experiences repeatedly reveal that if the Lord allows the cross, he also equips you with all the graces needed to bear it.

Although I do sometimes revert to old worrying habits, my faith has helped me turn more often (and more quickly) to Jesus. My prayer is that the hope I have found in him becomes your hope, too, as you read Scripture and open a prayerful dialogue with Jesus.

An Invitation to Ponder

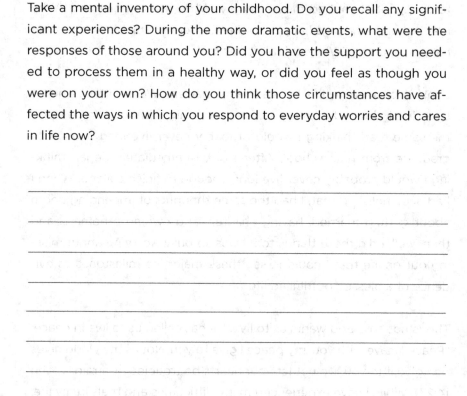

Take a mental inventory of your childhood. Do you recall any significant experiences? During the more dramatic events, what were the responses of those around you? Did you have the support you needed to process them in a healthy way, or did you feel as though you were on your own? How do you think those circumstances have affected the ways in which you respond to everyday worries and cares in life now?

_____

_____

_____

_____

_____

_____

_____

_____

_____

_____

_____

Connecting to Scripture

· ·

This section is my favorite part of the whole **Stay Connected** series. Pondering the Word of God took center stage in my reversion journey, deepening my faith in ways I never could have imagined.

Every time I sit with the Scriptures, the Holy Spirit fills me with a sense of his profound presence in my life. If you have ever longed to hear Jesus speak to you but feel that he remains silent, the Word of God is truly the best place to start. I recommend purchasing a Catholic Bible with an excellent commentary; you will find it an excellent complement to your reflections.

Take time to read each Scripture passage referenced below, and pay special attention to what the Holy Spirit is calling your attention to in each verse. Do not try to figure out a "right" response; this is your time with the Scriptures, and I promise that no one is going to grade your answers.

Relax and allow yourself to enjoy this time with the Word of God. Read each verse a few times, asking the Holy Spirit to guide your heart and mind to receive what he has prepared just for you. Use the space provided under each Scripture verse to note any inspirations or thoughts that come to you as you read. Share your thoughts with a small group or use your notes as a personal spiritual journal.

PRAYER TO THE HOLY SPIRIT BEFORE READING SCRIPTURE

Come, Holy Spirit, come. Fill me with every grace and blessing necessary to understand the message, prepared and waiting for me, in the Scriptures. May my time reading and contemplating the Word of God teach me not only to trust Jesus, but also to be open to the peace he longs to give me. Amen.

❧ Deuteronomy 31:6-8 _____

_____

_____

❧ Proverbs 3:5-8 _____

_____

_____

❧ Matthew 6:25-34 _____

_____

_____

❧ John 14:15-21, 26-27 _____

_____

_____

🖋 Romans 8:14–17 _____

_____

_____

_____

🖋 1 John 4:15–18 _____

_____

_____

Scripture Reflection

I think my absolute favorite line in Saint Matthew's Gospel is, "Can any of you by worrying add a single moment to your life-span?" (Matthew 6:27). The first time I read that, I laughed out loud. Saint Matthew, have we met?

Worry, to me, is an action verb. My thinking goes something like this: the more I worry about something, the less likely it is to happen. It's as if somehow my endless hours spent imagining all the different possible scenarios in my mind can change the future. Sure, in some instances, if it is a danger I am avoiding or a problem I can solve, considering the possibilities is not only positive but necessary. However, there are very few circumstances that fit that criteria. Usually, I am spinning my wheels for the sake of satisfying my worry receptors.

What to Do Instead of Worrying

Padre Pio wisely presents an effective method to navigate worry — pray. Specifically, he says, "Pray, hope and don't worry. Anxiety doesn't help at all. Our Merciful Lord will listen to your prayer."[3]

This seems straightforward, but first we'll have to make a habit of responding in this way. As you respond to anxiety with prayer more often, it will become your automatic response.

Scripture directs us 365 times to not worry, to not be afraid, and to not fear. It's as though the Holy Spirit wanted to give us a daily reminder about who is in control and who has our back. How powerful a lesson this is, to be reminded again and again to turn to the almighty and all-powerful God instead of focusing on what we lack.

My focus, which feels perpetually inward, should, instead, be outward and — even more importantly — upward. Away from myself, out to others, and always up to God. When I speak these negative thoughts out loud to a friend, spiritual director, or to the Lord, I am giving them to the light. Jesus is the Prince of Light. I am giving my worries and anxieties to Jesus so he can illuminate me with his light of truth.

On What Can I Rely?

"We have come to know and to believe in the love God has for us." These words from 1 John 4:16 always touch my heart in a special way. Another translation of this verse reads, "And so we know *and rely* on the love God has for us" (NIV, emphasis added). I love that word *rely*. It has been at the very core of my learning to trust God in all circumstances: instead of relying on my own devices and abilities, I surrender them to God's goodness, love, and incredible mercy.

"[F]or God all things are possible" (Matthew 19:26). These words are especially encouraging as I write this book, way past my deadline and fighting the fear that I will never finish it. It is a reasonable presumption that I do not possess all the skills, time, or focus to complete this task; and yet, I wholeheartedly believe that nothing is impossible for God.

As the writing of this manuscript extended weeks, then months, past my deadline, I grew increasingly anxious about the project. One night I found that I could not stop worrying long enough to fall asleep. I looked to heaven and prayed, "Lord, I cannot do this; I surrender it all to you. If you want it done, if it is your will, it will be done. With you, all things are possible." Within minutes, I was fast asleep. And if you are reading this, clearly the Lord answered that prayer and willed it to be done! Worrying did not finish the manuscript; trusting in the Lord, getting a good night's sleep, and using the gifts he has given me was the only way to complete this task.

In the Hands of God

In the reading from Matthew's Gospel, Jesus assures us of God's providence. We'll look at that reading in more detail in later chapters, but for now it is worth noting how Jesus calls us to remain in the present moment. The past cannot be changed, but the Lord can use our experiences to help us grow in holiness (without getting mired in hurt or trauma). We do not know what the future may hold, so there is no use in worrying about it; but we can trust that the direction of our lives is in the loving hands of God. If you're not sure about his trustworthiness, then use his amazing gift of hindsight to review the moments in your life where God has provided for you.

In the reading from John's Gospel, we are introduced to the promise of the Holy Spirit, sent by God to help us discern his holy will.

The Holy Spirit can light our way and bring us peace as we work to operate within God's great plan for us. The Holy Spirit is poured into our lives as grace; we merely need to cooperate with this divine gift.

Tapestry Weaving 101

The weaving of a tapestry is one of my favorite images of God working all things together for our good. If you only look at the backside of the tapestry — a tangle of interwoven threads — the image makes little sense. You might wonder about the artisan's skills or the intended design. It is not until you look at the front of the finished tapestry that you see its full beauty. On this side of heaven, your life will also be a tangle of crazy, seemingly random threads, but, in God's loving hands, the result will always be beautiful and good.

Invitation to Share

1. What does the word *surrender* mean to you? How does surrendering to God teach us to trust? Why do you think God might ask us to surrender to his will over our own?

_____

_____

_____

_____

_____

_____

2. Do you view worrying as an action verb? Have the Scriptures mentioned in this chapter given you any ideas for how you might handle your cares and concerns differently?

_____

_____

_____

_____

_____

_____

3. The saints, our brothers and sisters in faith, also had to navigate the trials and tribulations of this life and are now with God in heaven. Do you call upon the saints for assistance? If so, who are your go-to intercessors, or, as I would put it, who is in your "Saint Posse"? Unsure of who to ask for heavenly help? Simply do a Google search for "Who is the saint of ... " and discover a new heavenly friend. If you wish, share your results.

_____

_____

_____

_____

_____

_____

_____

Closing Prayer

Lord God, heavenly King, almighty God, and Father, weave the tapestry of my life according to your will, reminding me every day that your will for my life is good. You long to help me see that you will never abandon nor forsake me; it is your promise given to us through your Word. Help me to know that your words are truth and life and that I can trust in the Scriptures to teach me your ways. Let these words become part of my thought processes, so they can teach me to trust you.

I want to trust you with all my heart. I wish to invite you into those broken places where I allow worry to overcome me. I long to continually feel your love bring me peace — without doubt or fear disturbing it. All things are, indeed, possible with you, Lord, but I am just beginning this journey, and I'm going to need a massive outpouring of grace into my life and my heart to change all of these old thought processes into new, hopeful, and peaceful dialogues with you. Let this study and my time with it bear great fruit. Amen.

2: Building Trust through the Divine Physician

SEEKING PEACE: A SPIRITUAL JOURNEY

Opening Prayer

Almighty and ever-living God, guide me through this study to learn how to trust you and to accept your desire for me to have no anxiety at all. O Lord, guide my heart that I may avoid any thoughts that lead me to worry about my health and well-being. Show me how to be mindful of my body and the world around me without worrying needlessly about my future and the many things in this world I cannot control.

Lord, let my body worship and glorify you as I enjoy my good health when I have it and turn to you for healing and hope when I am sick. Fill my heart with the desire to care for my body as a temple of the Holy Spirit, gratefully enjoying the blessings you give your people. I want to appreciate the gift of technology and its ability to connect me with people throughout the world without becoming overwrought with fear or anxiety.

Lord, thank you for the gift of our guardian angels, who faithfully guide and guard us as ministers of your protection and peace. Thank you, Lord, for all the heavenly intercessors you provide for us in the saints. Help me to build a friendship with them so that I may ask for their assistance. Fill my heart with

23

peace, knowing that my prayers always reach you and are answered according to your divine will.

Let me not grow anxious in waiting for a response to my prayer. Help me remain confident that you plan for my good and never for my woe. Permit me to not fear what I cannot control but, instead, to relax in your love, staying ever present in the moment without drifting fearfully into the future. May I always stand firmly in the present, in your truth and in your love. Amen.

On My Heart

_____

_____

_____

_____

_____

_____

_____

_____

_____

_____

_____

_____

_____

_____

_____

_____

How My Fear of Death Stole My Life

Nothing triggers my anxiety like the possibility of death. Ironically, this fear of death has often gotten in the way of living life as fully as God intends! Let me give you some examples.

Scrolling through Instagram one Sunday afternoon, I paused at the image of a young woman identified as a loving mother of two young children, a successful writer, and a motivational speaker in Christian ministry. This information was immediately followed by an unexpected, "Rest in peace, faithful servant." _Wait, what!?_ Although I had never heard of this beautiful woman before, those words chilled me to the core. My body quickly went into what I call "anxiety response," when a wave of adrenaline floods my body, my stomach flutters, my face flushes, my hands tingle, and sometimes I even feel faint.

It's the perfect example of the type of news story that triggers my anxiety. This beautiful young woman was working hard to spread the Word of God when, out of nowhere, she got an infection, and within days she had died. Immediately my brain notes how much she had accomplished in her life: marriage, kids, a successful writing career, and a global ministry. All of these are amazing things, but here's how my anxious mind processed this social media post: _Don't accomplish your goals or you will die. If you never accomplish what you have been put here on earth to do, maybe you will live longer._

I am confident that this is not how life works, but that is how my worry-brain works. As a result, I often put off what I need to get done. Even though I recognize the personal and professional detriment of this behavior, I still fall into it more often than I care to admit.

Here's another example. In my senior year of high school, I was hit by a drunk driver on my way to school. Praise God, my dad made sure his newly licensed seventeen-year-old driver had a tank for a car. Although I foolishly wasn't wearing a seatbelt, my guardian angel pulled out the big save. My car was totaled, but I miraculously walked away from this horrific crash with only a few cuts and a broken nose.

But at the scene of the accident I heard a policeman tell my mother, "Your daughter is very fortunate. We had an accident just like this last week, and that young girl didn't survive." Far from reassuring me, his comment only intensified my anxiety. As a result, instead of celebrating the miracle of my survival, my takeaway was a paralyzing fear of being in a car.

Remembering Who Is in Control

At the core of my fear of being ill or injured, I believe, is my fear of not being in control of what is happening around me. I am the person who flips to the last page of a book to see how it ends before I will read it. I like knowing what is coming next. I am not adventurous. I want the complete game plan, and, quite honestly, I want a game plan filled with nothing but easy plays.

And yet, while stressful situations still trigger my anxiety response, I have learned to remember that God is always bigger than my fears. As the Veggie Tales would sing, "God is bigger than the Boogie Man." I may not be in control of what is happening around me, but God is.

As a result, today I routinely travel alone, fly across the country, and try extraordinary new experiences (even when they petrify me).

How am I able to do this? By practicing my faith and cooperating with God's grace. More concretely, one technique that I have found to be especially helpful is to be ready with a Scripture verse that reminds me that God loves me and watches over me. Is there a Scripture verse that brings you comfort whenever you read or hear it? God's Word can empower you to do what seems impossible, by trusting in his goodness and living courageously ... despite your fears.

No Rose Gardens

It's important for me to remember that handing control over to God means accepting the fact that I won't always see or understand his purposes, and that's okay.

I often try to convince God of the best outcome (according to my perspective) in every situation. Although my prayers cannot manip-ulate God, I try to remember that he is a loving Father, who will re-spond with love, even if he doesn't let me glimpse the last page of his plan. His promise is simple and sweet: "We know that all things work for good for those who love God, who are called according to his pur-pose" (Romans 8:28).

To paraphrase the old Lynn Anderson song from the 1970s, God never promised us a rose garden. Checking all the "Catholic boxes" or being faithful in prayer does not guarantee our lives will proceed without incident. Nor does it mean God will answer our prayers according to our preferred outcome. Just think of all the beautiful people you have prayed for whose healing took a long time to come, or maybe never came. Still, God is love and God is good. Holding onto that truth allows us to trust that the person we prayed for received God's healing love, even if it was not in the way we preferred.

An Invitation to Ponder

Do you spend more time on WebMD researching symptoms than an actual doctor would? Do stories on the news or on social media trigger anxiety or panic attacks? How do you bring health concerns — your own or those of others — to the Lord? Do you prayerfully submit to his will or find yourself begging for mercy against a diagnosis you may not even have? What change can you implement today to approach the future secure in the love of God?

_____

_____

_____

_____

_____

_____

_____

_____

_____

_____

_____

Connecting to Scripture

PRAYER TO THE HOLY SPIRIT BEFORE READING SCRIPTURE

Come, Holy Spirit, come. Fill me with every grace and blessing necessary to understand the message, prepared and waiting for me, in the Scriptures. May my time reading and contemplating the Word of God teach me not only to trust Jesus but also to be open to the peace he longs to give me. Amen.

❧ Matthew 9:19–22 _____

_____

_____

❧ Mark 8:31–9:1 (cf. Matthew 16:24–28; Luke 9:22–27) _____

_____

_____

_____

❧ Romans 5:3–5 _____

_____

_____

_____

❧ 2 Corinthians 12:5–10 _____

_____

_____

⮾ Ephesians 6:10–18 _____

_____

_____

⮾ James 5:13–15 _____

_____

_____

Scripture Reflection

"Courage, daughter! Your faith has saved you" (Matthew 9:22). The word *courage* is sometimes translated as "take heart" or "be encouraged," and the words *Your faith has saved you* is sometimes translated as "Your faith has made you well."

The choice to use the word *courage* is interesting, though, because to be courageous means to follow through or move ahead with an action despite the presence of fear. Courage is forging ahead even though you are unsure, nervous, or downright scared! If there were no fear, there would be no need for courage. The hemorrhaging woman has many reasons to fear: She is unclean, and touching Jesus, a respected teacher, could have dire consequences. She is desperate, with nothing to lose — but with enough hope to try one more thing. In this case, she needed the faith to believe that reaching out and touching Jesus would be worth the risk.

When faced with situations that scare you, what is your immediate reaction? Are you able to push through your fears and accomplish what needs to be done? What helps you be brave — desperation, faith, or a bit of both?

The hemorrhaging woman's act of faith touches Jesus, and not merely in the physical sense. When we reach out to Jesus in faith, it touches his heart. "Someone," Jesus says, "has touched me" (Luke 8:46). Can you almost hear the love in Jesus' voice? Picture him scanning the crowd, seeking to connect with this courageous person of faith. Then, the woman performs the most courageous act of all: although she is "trembling" (Luke 8:47), she steps forward and claims the touch as her own. Her brave willingness to enter into a dialogue with Jesus despite the possible negative consequences conveys an important lesson: if you have faith enough to pursue Jesus for help, you should then have courage enough to encounter him one on one.

What about "Unanswered" Prayers?

"[G]o in peace," Jesus tells the woman (Luke 8:48). And she can — because she received the cure she sought. She is leaving healed, whole, and very relieved. But what about all of us who come to Jesus and walk away unhealed? Are we still called to go in peace? Are we not touching his heart, not showing enough courage to warrant his healing us immediately as well?

Perhaps this is the moment Jesus would rebuke me, as he did Peter. Maybe this is when Jesus would turn and say, "Get behind me, Satan. You are thinking not as God does, but as human beings do" (Mark 8:33).

God's ways, as the prophet Isaiah tells us, are not our ways. His ways are higher (Isaiah 55:7–8). In the middle of the struggle, it can undoubtedly be hard to view God's higher ways as better. It is hard to accept "no" or "not yet" to our pleas for healing or help. The peace that comes from Jesus may sometimes be fleeting as worries crowd our minds. Some days, it is harder to calm the storms of "what-ifs" and allow God to have his way with our lives, trusting in his love even in illness, trial, or tragedy.

Like the hemorrhaging woman, I have been plagued by an ailment for years — dyshidrotic eczema, a disease marked by chronic inflammation with no known cure. When it flares up, it creates red, itchy, and swollen hands and feet.

Like Paul, I begged the Lord to take this affliction from me again and again (see 2 Corinthians 12:8). During flare-ups, the itch is maddening, and my hands and feet are practically incapacitated. On those days, I used to cry out, "Lord, please take this away!" Three years later, however, this "thorn" remains. While I still pray for a cure, Jesus consistently assures me that his grace is enough (2 Corinthians 12:9).

And what does that grace look like? On days when my hands are ripped bare and deformed, God teaches me to trust him, to see that relying on others can be a treasure, and to recognize that true beauty comes from within. My hands have been prayed over by a priest who survived the Rwandan genocide, by a Franciscan friar who brought me to tears by kissing my malformed hand, and by countless other faithful priests, deacons, and friends. My search for a cure has brought me to beautiful healing Masses, sent me on pilgrimages, and led me to venerate the relics of saints. While some might think my ongoing affliction is a failure of faith or that my prayers are a waste of time, I know I have received countless graces. Living each day with this disease has bestowed blessings upon me and my family in ways I cannot even begin to fathom.

Persevering in Prayer

Saint Paul teaches that affliction will bring blessings such as endurance, character, and hope (Romans 5:3–5). While I understand the merits of possessing such qualities, sometimes I want to be affliction free.

Saint Paul also teaches us to be constant in prayer, drawing our strength from the Lord. Pray at every opportunity and be watchful (Ephesians 6:18). One of my favorite ways of doing this is by praying a novena, a nine-day prayer of supplication that, according to tradition, is rooted in the nine days Mary and the apostles spent praying in the upper room while waiting for the promise of the Holy Spirit (Acts 1:4, 13–14). For me, the novena is a never-ending opportunity to see the Spirit at work — to see how he works through the situations bringing me angst, and to learn to trust in his goodness instead of being conquered by doubt and fear. Doubt and fear are tactics of the evil one to keep us captive, instead of allowing us to embrace the freedom Jesus came to give us.

More than thirty years ago, I was introduced to the novena of Saint Thérèse of Lisieux. While most novenas last nine days, this one is only five days long. I love that God knows my impatient character and blessed me with this speedy version! Another thing I love about this novena is that, while she was still alive, Saint Thérèse promised to shower the world in roses from heaven. Often, people who pray this novena receive a rose as a sign that their prayer has been heard. This doesn't mean your petition will be granted exactly as you expect, of course; it is just a consolation.

In the time before my husband's ordination to the diaconate, I prayed that the five of us would be healthy for the big day. I asked for a rose each day for each one of us, and each day, Saint Thérèse seemingly obliged my request. Imagine my bewilderment, then, when we all became sick with colds a week before the ordination! I was baffled until I realized the timing could not have been more perfect. Our immune systems were bolstered by our bout with the sniffles, and we were, indeed, all healthy for Kevin's big day!

Now, I am a bit of a brat because I ask Saint Thérèse to send me *purple* roses. My logic is that because pink and red roses are so common, I might mistake seeing one as an answer to prayer when it is just a coincidence. Yes, I know the logic of this is flawed, but still, each time I pray this novena, I ask for my purple rose.

Once, I was praying about an extra-long trip that was making me especially anxious. I really wanted some sign that my prayers had been heard. On the morning of the fifth day of my Saint Thérèse novena, I logged onto Facebook and was immediately greeted by a rose. It looked light purple, but the description called it light pink; glancing heavenward, I asked Thérèse for a darker rose, please. A few moments later, there was another rose in an online florist advertisement. This rose was much darker in color, and, while it looked deep plum, the description listed it as black.

"Thérèse," I finally asked out loud, "you know I am a hot mess about this trip. Can you please send me a no-doubt-about-it Crayola-purple rose, please?"

I logged into Instagram, and the first image to pop up was a perfectly purple rose. You can't make this stuff up. The trip was not without a few bumps, but my anxiety was kept at bay thanks to that purple rose.

"Do What You Can, and I Will Do the Rest"

Of course, it wasn't the purple rose itself that gave me strength and peace on that trip. My strength to overcome my sometimes-paralyzing fears comes from the Lord. It comes from reading and holding close to my heart the words of my Lord in the Scriptures. The grace of God is enough for me in all circumstances.

Jesus once said to a fretting Saint Faustina, "Do whatever you can in this matter; I will accomplish everything that is lacking in you. You know what is within your power to do; do that."[4] The Lord needs to say nothing more; this is the secret sauce to trusting God in the darkness and the great unknown. Do what you can — pray, read Scripture, and participate in the grace of the sacraments. But most importantly, allow God to do what he does best — be God.

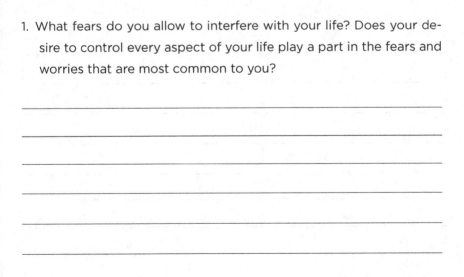

Invitation to Share

1. What fears do you allow to interfere with your life? Does your desire to control every aspect of your life play a part in the fears and worries that are most common to you?

_____

_____

_____

_____

_____

_____

2. How can the cross be a necessary part of being a disciple of Jesus?

_____

_____

_____

_____

_____

_____

_____

_____

3. Have you ever prayed for a miracle for yourself or someone else? What was the outcome? Were you able to see God's plan in the outcome, even if it differed from what you were praying for?

_____

_____

_____

_____

_____

_____

_____

_____

Closing Prayer

Lord, I want to touch your heart with my faith. I want to be the woman who pushes through every obstacle to reach out to you as the Divine Physician and Lover of My Soul. I can become so overwhelmed by circumstances that I forget that you are waiting to shield me against the arrows of despair and consuming worry. Knowing that you love me more than anything, and knowing that, even if I were the only one on earth, you still would have died for my soul should inspire peace and hope within me.

Our earthly dwelling is wrought with many frightening diseases, accidents, and circumstances beyond our control, but thankfully this world is not our home. The tragedies that happen here are not to define who I am in you. It feels like an attack of the devil to spend all that time and energy worrying about what might be, instead of living and enjoying the present. How I long to live in the hope of heaven, while focused on the here and now.

Lord, help me to give my best to those around me even when it means carrying my cross. Thank you for revealing to me that I never bear any burden alone; this knowledge brings joy to my heart. Peace and joy are two of the greatest gifts you offer us, especially the glorious peace that surpasses all understanding. I want to learn to trust you more and worry less. Inspire my heart to know and rely on the love that you have for me. Amen.

3: Building Trust through Wisdom and Surrender

SEEKING PEACE: A SPIRITUAL JOURNEY

Opening Prayer

Almighty and ever-living God, guide me through this study to learn how to trust you and to accept your desire for me to have no anxiety at all. O Lord, guide my heart in letting go of my own plans, trusting that yours are infinitely better than any I could even begin to dream.

In the secular world, surrender is a sign of defeat or weakness. But you teach us that submission to you is actually a sign of strength, courage, and victory. I long to remain faithful to your ways so I might be victorious over my anxiety. Help me to trust your plan for my good and your promise to bring forth blessings in every situation, especially when the things seem bleak and hopeless. My hope will always be in you because that hope is never misplaced.

With faith, I will hold tightly to the covenant you make with your people. You shall forever be our God, and we shall forever be your children.

Your generous love truly overwhelms me. I should not be surprised by it. For if I know how to give my children good things, how much more do you know how to provide good things for your children? The ultimate good you long to offer us when our life here is complete is an eternal crown of glory and an entrance into paradise — our heavenly abode! Amen.

On My Heart

_____

_____

_____

_____

_____

_____

_____

_____

_____

_____

_____

_____

_____

Letting Go

In my first **Stay Connected Journal,** *The Gift of Invitation: 7 Ways Jesus Invites You to a Life of Grace,* I shared the story about how God spoke to me during a Rosary walk. Just as I was imploring God to reveal what he wanted from me, a tractor-trailer with the word FIDELITY emblazoned across its side passed right in front of me. The timing was far too coincidental to not be from God — a classic "godcidence" moment.

God was simply asking me to be faithful — an important lesson, especially during the difficulties we were encountering at the time.

So, you want me to be faithful, Lord? I think I can do that. In the last five years, I have done my best to honor that request by being committed to the teachings of the Church, participating in the liturgy, paying close attention to the Scriptures, and diving into an abundance of spiritual reading. I have tried to learn as much as I can, praying to be open to the movement of the Spirit to teach me how to remain continually faithful.

Yet, my fears still rage within me. When I look at the difficult circumstances of other people's lives, it can be hard to believe God really wants good for us: a young person gets sick and dies; a father dies in an accident while picking up his son from a friend's house; a young mother dies during childbirth; a neighbor's home burns to the ground. Can these things really be used to bring about a good?

These are the things that haunt me, things that I can't reconcile in my mind. If God is so good, why do so many bad things happen, especially to really good people? *If I just hold tight to the reins of my life,* I think, *perhaps I can avoid suffering.* I teasingly told my editor that this book should have been titled *Waiting for the Other Shoe to Drop* because that is how I often think. As soon as something good happens, I start looking for something bad to follow on its heels. My grandmother used to say, "Don't get too happy, or you'll just tempt sadness to follow close behind." True story.

A God Who Keeps Promises

These questions were on my heart one day as I was driving home from adoration. *Lord, what do you want from me?* I asked. *How do I know you will keep your promise to me?* Just as I finished those last words, yet another truck passed in front of me; this one read, KEEPING PROMISES. The funny thing is that this happened on the very same road where God had sent me the Fidelity truck not so long before.

Seeing a truck with the words KEEPING PROMISES just as I am praying to believe in God's fidelity affirms for me not only that the veil between heaven and earth is thin but also that God is real and he is listening. In fact, the Fidelity truck just passed the house as I was writing these very words! Perhaps that's a sign that, as you read this book, the Holy Spirit will touch your heart to remain faithful as well.

What a blessing that we have a God who keeps his promises! How, then, can we not respond with humility and trust, in obedience to his teachings and his commandments? God will never ask the impossible from us; even in the things we think are difficult, Matthew's Gospel reminds us that "for God all things are possible" (Matthew 19:26). Yes, I want to hold on to control; I want to know what's coming next; I want to be the one who makes the decisions in my life. But I am not God. I cannot see all at once, the present along with the future; I do not know what is truly best for me.

Our Father Knows Best

The image of God as loving Father is helpful here. Sometimes I think about my children's willfulness, especially when they were toddlers. They were often convinced that they knew what was best for them. In some cases, what they wanted was fine, but perhaps the timing wasn't great. I didn't mind allowing my children to enjoy candy now and then, but I wouldn't hand it over at three in the morning, no matter how loudly they insisted on it. Other times, what they wanted was simply not good for them, such as when they didn't want to wear their seatbelts. Yet I knew they needed to put up with the discomfort of the seatbelt because of the safety it brought them.

In a similar way, God, my heavenly Father, always knows what is best for me, while I, being a "toddler" in the faith, often do not. This analogy gives me the courage to surrender to God's will.

To be able to defer to God as a loving Father brings me great peace. Instead of worrying about all the things that are out of my control, I just focus on what I can do, knowing that my Father in heaven loves me and keeps his promises.

How many things are we holding on to, trying to manipulate and control ... yet when we "let go and let God," they seem to work themselves out? Sometimes I will find an old to-do list with items left undone. It's incredible how the world kept turning despite those unfinished tasks! Maybe it was even a blessing that I didn't waste my time and energy on those things.

We need to begin every day with prayer so we are poised to allow the Lord to guide our steps. Proverbs beautifully articulates the connection between our plans and the Lord's care for us: "The human heart plans the way, but the Lord directs the steps" (Proverbs 16:9). Now that's a directive I can hang my hat on — waking up, praying, and giving my day to God, knowing he will guide my steps.

An Invitation to Ponder

Are you an optimist or pessimist by nature? Do you struggle to enjoy the highlight moments of your life for fear of what might follow? Do you have a relative, as I did, who warns you about being overly confident and happy because your circumstances could change all too quickly? What do you believe the Father's response would be to your reluctance to fully enjoy his gifts?

_____

_____

_____

_____

_____

_____

_____

_____

_____

_____

_____

_____

Connecting to Scripture

PRAYER TO THE HOLY SPIRIT BEFORE READING SCRIPTURE

Come, Holy Spirit, come. Fill me with every grace and blessing necessary to understand the message, prepared and waiting for me, in the Scriptures. May my time reading and contemplating the Word of God teach me not only to trust Jesus but also to be open to the peace he longs to give me. Amen.

❧ Psalm 62:2-3, 6-9 _____

_____

_____

❧ Isaiah 55:6-9 _____

_____

_____

❧ Jeremiah 29:11-13 _____

_____

_____

❧ Luke 10:38-42 _____

_____

_____

❧ 2 Corinthians 1:3-7 _____

_____

_____

֍ Philippians 4:4–9_____

_____

_____

Scripture Reflection

Psalm 62 speaks serious comfort to my heart: Your foes are destroyed when you trust. Your joy is equal to the amount of trust you are willing to give God. Joy in the Lord is not fleeting happiness. Joy remains unshakable when rooted in our love and trust of the Lord. In the blink of an eye, my happiness can disappear, just as when I prance into the kitchen for a sweet treat to discover someone else beat me to it!

"Pour out your hearts to God our refuge!" (Psalm 62:9). Sure, losing out on a sweet treat might not seem to require God's intervention. However, if you were counting on that muffin to ease a broken heart, it undoubtedly qualifies as a better plan. Pouring out her heart is precisely what Martha of Bethany did when she became exasperated by her sister's seemingly lazy behavior when Jesus and his disciples came to visit (Luke 10:38–42).

"Do you not care?" Martha asked Jesus as her sister, Mary, sat at his feet. Does it not seem that sometimes we struggle more than others? We work forty-plus hours a week to make ends meet, barely. Meanwhile, our neighbors take relaxing Caribbean vacations, send their children debt-free to the best colleges, and will retire at sixty-two, and we're just wondering if we will retire before we die.

Jesus' disciples posed the same type of question on the boat during the storm: "Teacher, do you not care that we are perishing?" (Mark 4:38).

How does Jesus respond to these questions? To Martha, he says: "Martha, Martha, you are anxious and worried about many things. There is need of only one thing" (Luke 10:41–42). And to the disciples he says, "Why are you terrified? Do you not yet have faith?" (Mark 4:40).

The "one thing" that we need is to have faith in Jesus. Consider Peter, invited by Jesus to come out to him on the water. As soon as he took his eyes off Jesus, he began to sink (Matthew 14:30). How many times have we taken our eyes off Jesus, felt like we were going under, and become completely overwhelmed by our circumstances? How I can relate to Peter! In the storms of finances, family concerns, and the world at large, I often lose sight of Jesus.

We Are Never, Ever Abandoned

Oh, how I can relate to Martha and Peter! How many times have I looked at the injustice, confusion, and storms in my own life, then turned to heaven and uttered, "Do you not care?" This feeling of being alone in the world, especially during moments when I need God the most, has been a constant source of anxiety in my life. Although I know of God's promise to provide the Holy Spirit as our guide, counselor, and Paraclete, there are still moments when I struggle to hear his voice or feel his presence.

Yes, the Holy Spirit will not leave us to fend for ourselves, nor abandon us in our time of need. But I had a hard time believing this promise, in part because of my gross misunderstanding of the words Jesus spoke from the cross: "My God, my God, why have you forsaken me?" (Mark

15:34). I'd been wrongly taught that Jesus' suffering on the cross was so great that the Father could not bear to look upon his Son in that state and looked away.

This could not be any further from the truth. God cannot go against his nature; if he tells us he'll never abandon nor forsake us (see Deuteronomy 31:6), he means he will never, ever abandon us. There is no circumstance or situation in which God is not with us. Therefore, the Father did not abandon Jesus during his Passion. Instead, as we look more closely at the words Jesus speaks, we learn that God not only is there, but also will bring victory (good) into everything, including our personal crosses.

The witnesses of the crucifixion would have been very familiar with the Psalms. They would have known that Jesus' words were quoted from Psalm 22, known as The Prayer of an Innocent Person. Although the psalm begins as a lament, it ends with a cry of victory. Listen to the latter verses of Psalm 22:

> You who fear the Lord, give praise!
> All descendants of Jacob, give honor;
> show reverence, all descendants of Israel!
> For he has not spurned or disdained
> the misery of this poor wretch,
> Did not turn away from me,
> but heard me when I cried out.
>
> (Psalm 22:24–25)

How glorious the plight of the man of whom David sings! How glorious the victory of Jesus from the cross! And how glorious our victory over the worries of this world when we stand with Jesus and place our anxieties at the foot of the cross!

Only when we read Jesus' words in light of the entire psalm do we recognize that these words were meant to teach us an important lesson: God is always at work in our lives, especially in times of trouble.

We Are Children of God

Just as the Father did not abandon Jesus on the cross, neither will he abandon us, because, by Jesus' death and resurrection and through the waters of Baptism, we have been adopted as children of God: "For you did not receive a spirit of slavery to fall back into fear, but you received a spirit of adoption, through which we cry, 'Abba, Father!' The Spirit itself bears witness with our spirit that we are children of God" (Romans 8:15–16).

Here's the magnitude of this promise. The Code of Canon Law states: "Children who have been adopted in accordance with the civil law are considered the children of that person or those persons who have adopted them."[5] This earthly definition of adoption is exactly what God intends for us in his heavenly family.

Nothing burns my toast more than someone meeting my daughter, Faith, and asking if I have any children of my own. Others sigh at our situation and comment, "I could never love a child that wasn't mine." No wonder people struggle to accept that they are beloved children in the family of God! Before we can believe we have been adopted as children of God, we must believe in adoption as a viable means to become family here on earth.

Invitation to Share

1. What type of things bring you comfort? Are they physical items or behaviors you find yourself turning to when distressed? Can you use any of those to grow closer to Christ?

_____

_____

_____

_____

_____

_____

_____

_____

2. After reading Saint Paul's armor of God analogy, which piece of armor do you feel you need to strengthen? Why? Which piece of armor do you feel you have properly fortified?

_____

_____

_____

_____

_____

_____

_____

3. Do you believe in God's promise to bring good into your life from all circumstances?

_____

_____

_____

_____

_____

_____

Closing Prayer

Lord God, heavenly king, almighty God, and Father, I know I will find joy through surrender to your amazing love. The troubles of this world are no match for your victory over sin and death. How easily I can lose my peace when I lose sight of you! But when I remain in you, I find joy.

Your word is peace and light in my dark thoughts. Please, Lord, continue to shine your love into those moments and keep me from drowning in my inward, negative thoughts. Yes, there will be difficulties, but you have revealed through your passion, death, and resurrection that you have overcome the troubles of this world. Do not let my heart grow weary in seeking you among the thickets and brambles of financial, physical, or emotional concerns. Although I may not be able to see you, you are ever present.

You are my comfort. You are my hope. You, I am slowly learning, are my all in all. Adopted into your family through my Baptism, may I claim my rightful place as your beloved daughter, sister, and friend. Let this study and my time with it bear great fruit. Amen.

4: Building Trust through Providential Care

Opening Prayer

Almighty and ever-living God, guide me through this study to learn how to trust you and to accept your desire for me to have no anxiety at all. O Lord, guide my heart in relying on your providential care. Teach me how to love you above all else and how to live in this world but not of it. Lord, I wish to be a good steward of all the blessings you give me. I want to use my gifts and talents for your glory, as well as for providing for my family and community.

Lord, help me to learn to distinguish between what my family needs and what my family wants. Help me to learn how to be content with what I have and to see that you have provided all we need. Please shield my eyes from peering in envy at the blessings my neighbors receive. Instead, let me rejoice in their good fortune. Remind me often of your generosity in my own life.

Lord, help me to be vigilant of the evil that wants to steal my peace by skewing my focus on this world. Let my joy be complete in you, and, although you are delighted to provide me with material belongings, let them not become the center of my life.

Instead of becoming indebted in order to have a life that I believe will bring me happiness, let me stay focused on the treasure that is a relationship with you. May my eternal warehouse be filled with blessings that will never fade. Lord, I've spent so many years trying to be happy by surrounding myself with false idols I thought would make me happy, but the happiness they brought was fleeting.

Lord, I desire to be content with what I have, worshiping only you and not things. Scripture says the love of money is the root of all evil; may I, then, love you above all things, leaving earthly goods and wealth in their proper place. Amen.

On My Heart

_____

_____

_____

_____

_____

_____

_____

_____

_____

Money Matters

I'm a great fan of comfortable living. I like having stuff — not fancy, expensive stuff, but simple, modern conveniences. I am also very impatient. Once I discover something fitting my comfortable-stuff criteria, I want to buy it — immediately. Online shopping must be the single worst invention for my impulsive nature. As I sit at my computer, clicking my way through an online store, it is easy for me to forget I am spending actual money. There was a time in my life that I could drop a hundred dollars (or more) in a few minutes, regardless of whether we could afford it. Unwilling to admit that my anxieties were paralyzing me, I spent years self-medicating with shopping.

At that time, stuff equaled security for me. I figured that if I could surround myself with things and give my family everything they wanted, then all would be fine. This warped sense of protection, coupled with poor money-management skills, finally caught up with me. After many years of borrowing from one creditor to pay another, that precariously balanced tower of debt finally toppled. Our debts far exceeded our income and credit — so much so that I had lost track of the exact amount.

Coming Clean

My anxiety about paying the bills was usurped only by my fear of revealing everything to my husband, from whom I'd kept our financial woes secret. (Kevin had entrusted me to handle our finances, which made the secrecy easier.) I begged the Lord to rescue me from this horrible mess and received a gentle but firm internal response that I just knew came from the Lord: unless I told Kevin everything, God was not coming to my aid.

It took me a while to get up the courage to tell my husband that I had been secretly hiding debt from him for the last twenty-five years. When I finally told him, he forgave me — but we still had to navigate some treacherous financial waters.

This all took place at the end of fall, just as our turn to host Thanksgiving dinner was approaching. Our bank account was empty. We had no more credit — and no money to purchase food for Thanksgiving dinner. Embarrassed, I refused to reach out to our families for help. I went to my knees and begged the Lord for his assistance. I knew it would take a miracle for us to get through November.

The Fidelity Truck Rides Again

After prayer, I decided to call the bank. I had been a customer for thirty years; certainly, I reasoned, they could do something to help. We needed only a *little* extra reserve credit to buy our feast. During my brief conversation with the bank, four Fidelity trucks drove past my window. First a Fidelity truck passed from the left, then came one from the right, then a big one, then a smaller one.

But despite what felt like a sure sign that the bank was the answer to my prayer, the manager explained there was nothing she could do. I hung up the phone, put my head in my hands, and said, "Lord, I surrender. I have no idea how you're going to fix this or help us, but I do trust in you."

A few moments later, a friend messaged me complaining about how her church, as a token of their appreciation, had given her family a giant frozen turkey. She had no idea what she was going to do with this monstrous thing because they would be traveling for Thanksgiving. Tears welled in my eyes as a crazy sense of relief rushed through my body. I explained our situation and humbly asked if we could have the turkey. We met up a short while later in a coffee shop parking lot. Pulling our cars side-by-side, we opened our trunks and transferred the goods from one cooler to another. We still laugh when we reminisce about how God answered my prayer in such an unusual way.

Multiplication of the Turnips and Rutabagas

Never outdone in his generosity, the Lord had a few more surprises in store for me. Upon returning from "The Great Turkey Caper," a piece of paper on the shelf caught my attention. A new organic garden had opened down the road, and, in exchange for using a small portion of our front yard for a sign, they were offering us shares in the garden. The paper reminded me we had not cashed in our shares for several months.

Much to my delight, the garden stand remained open until December 1. The young woman behind the counter added up my shares and joked that we had enough for "quite a feast." I filled my cart with potatoes, carrots, turnips, and rutabagas. I didn't even know what those last two things were, but I knew you could cook them. I cried the whole way home, overwhelmed by God's goodness. My family took care of the rest of the meal, and I even found a bottle of wine on the shelf. God had taken care of our necessities; I had been steadfast in prayer, and he had been faithful in his promise to care for us.

Better Than a Lottery Ticket

One of the most miraculous moments came when I went to my bank on November 30 prepared to beg for leniency with the overdrafts I was sure we'd incurred. We had had to pay an unexpected house bill, plus a creditor unwilling to wait for their payment. Certain that things were as bleak as they could be, I sat down in the branch manager's office and asked her to assess the damage. As she scrolled and scrolled through the account, her face scrunched up in confusion. Not only had we not bounced any checks, we had $100 left in the account! I briefly wondered whose money we possibly stole or if she would soon discover a bank error.

Encouraged by these Thanksgiving blessings, Kevin and I began to pray together for the Lord to show us the way out. While we would have happily accepted a winning lottery ticket, God, instead, sent help that would make a lasting difference — someone to teach us how to manage our money. At the time, I had a radio show, and my first guests in January were financial planners Jon and Evelyn John Bean, who wrote *Navigating Your Finances God's Way* for Compass Catholic Ministries. After hearing our story, they offered to give us their financial planning workbook in exchange for me blogging a short series of articles about our experience with the program. God always has a perfect plan.

An Invitation to Ponder

At some point in life, everyone worries about paying for something. When have you needed to rely on God's providence in your life? What was the most remarkable lesson you learned from that? If you have not had your own experience with divine providence, have you seen it at work in another person's life?

_____

_____

_____

_____

_____

_____

_____

_____

_____

_____

_____

Connecting to Scripture

PRAYER TO THE HOLY SPIRIT BEFORE READING SCRIPTURE

Come, Holy Spirit, come. Fill me with every grace and blessing necessary to understand the message, prepared and waiting for me, in the Scriptures. May my time reading and contemplating the Word of God teach me not only to trust Jesus but also to be open to the peace he longs to give me. Amen.

❀ Psalm 63:2-6 _____

_____

_____

〽 Matthew 6:19–21 _____

_____

_____

〽 Luke 16:1–13 _____

_____

_____

〽 1 Timothy 6:17–19 _____

_____

_____

〽 Hebrews 13:5–6 _____

_____

_____

〽 1 Peter 5:5b–11 _____

_____

_____

The parable Jesus tells about the dishonest steward in Luke's Gospel has always confused me. That is why I own a Bible that has an excellent Catholic commentary. My *Didache Bible*[6] explains that the master in the parable admired the unjust steward not because he was lazy and dishonest, but because he demonstrated a resourceful craftiness. In a similar way, Christian disciples should use their earthly goods in a way that will ensure their salvation when those goods are taken away from them at death.

Practicing Detachment

That parable offers a powerful lesson in detachment, something I'm not very good at. For many years, I was attached to clothing and shoes, movies, and music CDs. I have boxes of these things packed away in my basement, yet I find it difficult to let them go. A few years ago, my house began to look like an episode of *Hoarders*. I found great comfort in keeping things, especially when those items held precious memories of my children being little. I had a hard time letting go of magazines too, feeling guilty that I hadn't even leafed through them.

These are all things that the moths will come and eat; they are not my treasure in heaven. I hope to find heaven filled with tiaras, fancy (perfect-fitting) dresses, and lots of books, along with a banquet filled with delicious foods I am no longer allergic to eating.

Detachment can be a problematic word, especially when your attachments are where you find solace and consolation. At different points in my life, I have found comfort in food, wine, and shopping. Those comforts were fleeting and, especially in the case of wine, not always so comforting in the end. Many years ago, as I looked around at the piles of things weighing me down, I made the tough, yet life-changing decision, to rent a dumpster. For an entire weekend, my husband and I sorted through all our stuff.

We had blessed many things forward through donations and the boys had held a yard sale, yet enough junk remained to fill a dumpster. It broke my heart to part with some of these objects. Ironically, the decision to detach became more natural with each discarded or donated item. I recycled, I reorganized, and I relied on the love of God to get me to a point where I could detach from these things. My understanding of what brings me happiness changed dramatically throughout the purging process until I finally realized that none of these earthly treasures contains the love, grace, or comfort present in my Lord and my God.

As the trash dumpster was hauled away, my home felt lighter, and so did I. I no longer had to continually relocate, trip over, or sift through my piles. Once they were gone, I realized that instead of comforting me, they had become a constant reminder of how I had used these things as a barricade between God and me when I had sought solace in shopping.

The Surplus of Your Heart

Jesus teaches, "It is more blessed to give than to receive" (Acts 20:35). One of my life goals is to be generous to a fault. My generosity, unfortunately, has long been tied to how my family is doing financially. But the Scriptures make it clear: your generosity should not come from your surplus but from your heart.

It's difficult to not think of the widow's mite in Luke's Gospel:

When he looked up he saw some wealthy people putting their offerings into the treasury and he noticed a poor widow putting in two small coins. He said, "I tell you truly, this poor widow put in more than all the rest; for those others have all made offerings from their surplus wealth, but she, from her poverty, has offered her whole livelihood." (Luke 21:1-4)

Honestly, I hesitate and outright struggle to hand over those last few pennies.

My giving, when done with the purest of intentions and through the counsel of the Holy Spirit, seems to bless not only the recipient but my family as well. Likewise, when my giving has been purely for show or recognition, while it hopefully blessed the receiver, it came without a returned blessing.

True Generosity

Once I was visiting a Franciscan chapel for daily Mass. To my surprise, they passed a collection basket. I'd come to the chapel to pray for my family's dire financial circumstances. As the basket drew closer, I caressed the dollar in my purse. The bill was special to me, as it had come in response to a prayer that my family would make it through this hardship. I had clung to this dollar as a security blanket and a true gift from the Lord.

Finally, decision time came. I placed the lone dollar bill in the basket, offering a whispered prayer, "Jesus, I trust in you." That evening as I was changing my clothes for bed, a dollar fell out of my pants pocket. I laughed out loud and then quickly apologized to Jesus. How, Lord, could I ever doubt your unparalleled generosity?

A return on investment (so to speak) should never be the motivation to be generous. The fact that I have witnessed God's repeated generosity is merely an observation. If that were not reason enough to guard my intentions, these words from Jesus sure are:

> "[But] take care not to perform righteous deeds in order that people may see them; otherwise, you will have no recompense from your heavenly Father. ... But when you give alms, do not let your left hand know what your right is doing, so that your almsgiving may be secret. And your Father who sees in secret will repay you." (Matthew 6:1, 3–4)

Being generous is a journey ... one that is traveled through the practice of virtue, prayer, and of course, grace!

Giving from Our Poverty

Giving generously from your heart especially when you are pulling from depleted resources can be very difficult. It is a journey to trust in God's providence and in the blessings of being generous. There have been many times when sharing our treasure has not come easy, although I must admit that responding to those calls to be generous from our poverty became easier when I was able to witness the fruits of my donations.

Real generosity comes without reward. It comes without promises or assurances of reward. Real generosity comes from allowing Christ to live in and through you. It remembers from whom all good gifts come (James 1:17) and to whom we owe everything. Real generosity is a paying forward of the invaluable gifts that God has bestowed generously upon us — hope, faith, and, most notably, love.

Invitation to Share

1. When you look around your home, do you see just what you need or an excess of what you wanted? Are there things you wish you had? Would those things change your life if you had them? How will you feel if you never acquire them?

_____

_____

_____

_____

_____

_____

_____

_____

_____

_____

2. In your trials, where does your consolation come from? If your consolation comes from God, explain how it looks in your life. You can reference a specific circumstance or speak in general terms. If not from God, from where or from whom does it come, and why?

_____

_____

_____

_____

_____

_____

_____

_____

_____

_____

3. Have you ever been faced with a difficult decision, especially a financial one, which required a total abandonment of your anxieties and
a complete trust in God's plan for you? Would asking for the grace
to detach help you to let go of some of your concerns or worries?

_____

_____

_____

_____

_____

_____

_____

_____

Closing Prayer

Lord God, heavenly king, almighty God, and Father, you are the giver of all good gifts; no one is as generous as you. I am trying to build up my treasure for heaven by living a life of faith and devotion to you. Help me to remember my future — both here and above; every single second is in your hands.

I need not worry about what I shall eat, drink, or wear. You know these needs and have already made provisions for me in each of them. May your words regarding your care and keeping of me become part of my thought processes, so they can continually teach me to trust you.

The birds in the air know of your goodness; why do I still struggle to believe in it? My faulty eyes see the burden of bills, work, and the increasing costs of living in this world. God, you did not create us with the earth as our final destination; we are made for so much more. I need not be worried or afraid; as a good and loving Father, you delight in providing for your children. Let this study and my time with it bear great fruit. Amen.

5: Building Trust through Devotions

SEEKING PEACE: A SPIRITUAL JOURNEY

Opening Prayer

Almighty and ever-living God, guide me through this study in learning how to trust and accept your desire for me to have no anxiety at all. O Lord, teach my heart to recognize all the remarkable ways the traditions and practices of the Catholic faith help me to ward off anxiety that threatens to overtake my thoughts. Your abundant grace made available in prayer, participation in the sacraments, and time spent in reading the Scriptures equips me for whatever I may encounter in my life.

Some days my rosary beads resemble worry beads as I work my way through the prayers. When my fears and concerns paralyze me, how grateful I am for the active prayer inherent in the Catholic faith. Prayer is an encounter with you, my Lord, and with each meeting in prayer, Word, or sacrament, your grace transforms me, even if just the smallest amount.

Sitting in your real presence while in adoration of the Blessed Sacrament or engaged in the greatest prayer ever, the celebration of the Mass, peace is restored or maintained. Grace abounds where you are, and, when I am open to receiving it, that grace

abounds in me. How grateful I am, Lord, for the variety of ways you provide to move my thoughts from inward concerns to upward glory. You are a generous and loving God.

Lord, in prayer, I raise my heart and mind to you, opening communication and embarking on a journey of faith no one else offers. Your promises abound in the Scriptures; every page brings another joy. Help me to recall your nature: you cannot lie, and you cannot promise what you will not accomplish. I want to know your truths, so I am persevering in faith, always trusting in your goodness, mercy, and love. Amen.

On My Heart

The Church's Many Beautiful Devotions

"Prayer is the raising of one's mind and heart to God or the requesting of good things from God," according to Saint John Damascene (*Catechism*, 2559). While prayer may not change our circumstances, it always changes our heart. It brings us closer to God in a way that allows him to comfort us, guide us, and, occasionally, reveal his plan for us. At the very least, communication with God always brings peace.

The Catholic faith offers many beautiful devotions, each suited to the different communication styles of the faithful. God created each of us to be unique and unrepeatable; therefore, it stands to reason that he would provide a variety of ways to communicate with him.

The Rosary: School of Mary

The Rosary covers so many prayer experiences for me. It engages all my senses, giving my fingers something to fidget with, my mind something to contemplate, my ears something to listen to as I pray out loud, and, when I use my rose-scented rosary beads, it even employs my sense of smell. This prayer, which I struggled to include in my prayer life, has evolved into an invaluable gift.

The Rosary allows me to hold onto something, especially when I'm struggling. There have been times in my life when the words would not come, yet merely having in my hands this beautiful sacramental brought me comfort and hope. Saint John Paul II has called the Rosary "the school of Mary." Meditating upon the mysteries of the Rosary, we learn so much about who Jesus is and how he wants to be a part of our lives. Furthermore, when we reflect on the life of Jesus with Mary, we realize that, although she endured many adversities, she never lost her joy and hope. Praying with Mary to our Lord provides us an opportunity to grow in faith guided by a loving mother.

"The Rosary ends wars." These profound words were spoken by a priest during the closing remarks of a reflection day that I was attending. The statement stunned me, perhaps because we were on a military base at the time. My attention had been drifting, but, after that statement, Father had my full attention.

"The Rosary helps end wars," he went on to say, "not only wars in our world, as with the Fatima apparitions and World War I, but the many wars in our lives — those wars that rage within our hearts, our bodies, our families."

Praying the Rosary has helped me tame the wars raging within me — in my case, the wars of acute anxiety, ADHD, and insecurity. Physically, I battle chronic inflammation and disfiguring dyshidrotic eczema that leaves me feeling itchy, embarrassed, and uncomfortable. Some days, praying is difficult. Some days, I do not want to pray. Some days, when I feel particularly beaten down by my internal conflicts and physical afflictions, prayer seems like a futile task. There are days when I can only muster up enough strength to hold onto my rosary; it's my lifeline as I wait for the Blessed Mother to draw me under the loving protection of her mantle. I grasp my rosary to be comforted by the feel of the beads when the words of my prayer fail to come. Someone once told me that holding those beads is like holding Mary's hand. "Who doesn't love holding their momma's hand?" she added.

Sister Lucia dos Santos, one of visionaries of Fatima, once said:

> The Most Holy Virgin, in these last times in which we live, has
> given a new efficacy to the recitation of the rosary to such an
> extent that there is no problem, no matter how difficult it is,
> whether temporal or above all spiritual, in the personal life of
> each one of us, of our families ... that cannot be solved by the
> rosary. There is no problem, I tell you, no matter how difficult
> it is, that we cannot resolve by the prayer of the holy rosary.[7]

I love the reminder that among the many problems we face, none of
them are beyond the reach of God. We can never fathom God's plan
completely. His ways, the prophet Isaiah tells us, are not our ways; his
ways are higher than our ways, yet he does provide us the gift of the
Holy Spirit so that we can understand what we need to restore our
hearts to a place of peace. Through prayer, we do not fix ourselves;
rather, we set our gaze upon Jesus. Instead of seeking answers within
ourselves, we bring our problems to the only one who has the answers and who can comfort us when those answers are not what we
were hoping to hear.

The Daily Grace of the Sacraments

One of the most life-changing discoveries I've made about the Catholic faith has been realizing that the seven sacraments can be lived out
in the ordinary, everyday context of our lives. While some sacraments
may be "one and done" (such as Baptism and Confirmation), there is
an abundance of blessings available to the individual open to seeing
the seven sacraments as continual conduits of grace. Let's examine a
few of them further.

Baptism: The Grace to Grow in Faith

The *Catechism of the Catholic Church* has this to say about the sacrament of Baptism:

> Baptism is the sacrament of faith. But faith needs the community of believers. It is only within the faith of the Church that each of the faithful can believe. The faith required for Baptism is not a perfect and mature faith, but a beginning that is called to develop. (*Catechism*, 1253)

The reference to Baptism as "a beginning" leads me to understand that it *continues* in some way. Baptism is an entry into the Christian life, and faith comes from embracing the promises of this sacrament. The grace to grow to a mature faith comes from continually renouncing Satan and working to better understand what it means to believe in the Father, Son, and Holy Spirit. This embracing of our call to live the sacrament of Baptism is only the beginning of the daily blessings God has for us.

The Blessed Sacrament: Communion with Jesus

While the Eucharist is available daily, it is not always feasible for many people to attend daily Mass. We can still make a spiritual reception by reciting Saint Alphonsus Liguori's Act of Spiritual Communion:

> My Jesus,
> I believe that You are present in the Most Holy Sacrament.
> I love You above all things, and I desire to receive You into
>   my soul.
> Since I cannot at this moment receive You sacramentally,
>   come at least spiritually into my heart.

I embrace You as if You were already there and unite
myself wholly to You.
Never permit me to be separated from You.

Amen.

The *Catechism of the Catholic Church* speaks so beautifully about the sacraments that welcome us into the Church, the Body of Christ:

> "The faithful are born anew by Baptism, strengthened by the sacrament of Confirmation, and receive in the Eucharist the food of eternal life. By means of these sacraments of Christian initiation, they thus receive in increasing measure the treasures of the divine life and advance toward the perfection of charity." (*Catechism*, 1212)

The great moments in our faith journey, such as Baptism and Confirmation, may seem to be single events, but they prepare our hearts to receive the continuous gift of God's grace in our lives. We are nourished daily by the grace of Baptism and are able to call out to Jesus in every situation. These true treasures provide each person with a connection to God from which they can build a life of trust, a trust that removes fear and inspires hope and peace.

"I am confident of this, that the one who began a good work in you will continue to complete it until the day of Christ Jesus" (Philippians 1:6). The grace that was poured out in us through Baptism increases each time we receive the Eucharist and is brought to completion through the sacrament of Confirmation. How beautifully the sacraments of Christian initiation come together to strengthen and mature our faith! Embracing the fullness of these spiritual gifts within us, we can now go forward in living our Christian witness with confidence!

Furthermore, the Lord continues to nourish us with the Bread of Life throughout our journey:

> ✐ *in the reception of the Eucharist;*

> ✐ *in spiritual communion;*

> ✐ *in Eucharistic adoration; and*

> ✐ *in our baptismal call to share in Jesus' ministry as priest, prophet, and king.*

Holy Orders: Living the Call to Holiness

While most of the faithful are not be called to receive the sacrament of Holy Orders, all of the baptized share in Christ's priesthood and, thus, are able to fulfill the call to holiness "in all dimensions of their personal, family, social, and ecclesial lives" (*Catechism*, 941). We can also connect with this sacrificial sacrament by committing to pray for priests and deacons.

Matrimony: We Are Family

A devout and wise woman at my parish once twisted the wedding band on her ring finger and proclaimed that because of this ring, she is never without a sacramental. Sacramentals, while not conduits of grace in and of themselves, are reminders of God's grace in our lives. In this instance, wedding rings remind the married couple of the gift of grace which accompanies their sacramental bond. The *Catechism* teaches that through the sacrament of Matrimony, Christ dwells with the couple, strengthening them to "take up their crosses and so fol-low him, to rise again after they have fallen, to forgive one another, to bear one another's burdens, to 'be subject to one another out of reverence for Christ,' and to love one another with supernatural, tender, and fruitful love" (1642).

Single people may feel excluded from the grace of the sacrament of Matrimony. But Saint John Paul II reassures us that all are welcome in the "family" that is the Church: "No one is without a family in this world: the Church is a home and family for everyone ... " (*Catechism*, 1658).

We are the Body of Christ, united in our Baptism. Through that same Baptism, we share in the life of Christ. The grace God bestows upon a couple in Matrimony creates community when that couple goes forth not only to love one another but to bring that love into the whole Church.

Reconciliation: The Grace to Forgive

In the sacrament of Reconciliation, the Catholic Christian can learn not only to accept mercy but also to be merciful to others. Although we can receive the sacrament as often as we like, an outpouring of grace comes when we participate in the sacrament by practicing forgiveness every day. When we live this sacrament beyond the walls of the confessional, we not only enhance our relationship with God but also strengthen the entire body of Christ (*Catechism*, 1469).

Anointing: Sharing in the Suffering of Others

It may seem to be more difficult to find a way to live the sacrament of Anointing in our daily lives; however, turning to Scripture offers some insight.

In the parable of the Good Samaritan (Luke 10:30–37), Jesus describes how a Samaritan passing by the half-dead victim of a robbery stops to help him. "But a Samaritan traveler who came upon him was moved with compassion at the sight. He approached the victim, poured oil and wine over his wounds and bandaged them. Then he lifted him up on his own animal, took him to an inn and cared for him" (Luke 10:33–34).

At the conclusion of the parable, Jesus tells his listeners to "Go and do likewise" (Luke 10:37). When we go forth into the world and bring healing, help, and compassion, we perform the work of the sacrament of Anointing. While we don't place oil on people's heads or give them absolution, when we love like Jesus, especially those who are wounded physically, emotionally, or spiritually, we are sharing Christ's healing grace.

An Invitation to Ponder

What is your personal relationship with the Rosary? What war in your life would you like to ask the Lord, through the prayers of the Rosary, to mitigate or even completely remove?

_____

_____

_____

_____

_____

_____

_____

_____

_____

_____

_____

Connecting to Scripture

PRAYER TO THE HOLY SPIRIT BEFORE READING SCRIPTURE

Come, Holy Spirit, come. Fill me with every grace and blessing necessary to understand the message, prepared and waiting for me, in the Scriptures. May my time reading and contemplating the Word of God teach me not only to trust Jesus but also to be open to the peace he longs to give me. Amen.

Genesis 22:13–18 _____

_____

_____

Mark 9:14–29 _____

_____

_____

⁊ Acts 12:6 –16 _____

_____

_____

⁊ 1 Thessalonians 5:14-24 _____

_____

_____

⁊ Hebrews 10:35–39 _____

_____

_____

Scripture Reflection

Living a life trusting in God begins with having faith that he knows what the plan is, even when you don't completely understand how it will all play out. We trust in his wisdom and love, knowing that the Lord will provide in all our needs and believing in the abundant blessings to come from our humble obedience and surrender.

Genesis 22 and Acts 12 reveal a mysterious, beautiful gift each of us receives from God — angels. The Scriptures include numerous examples of the essential role angels play in God's plans. Angels aren't just for people living long ago; each of us is also given a guardian angel, our very own personal connection with God. Do you remember this child-hood prayer?

Angel of God,

my guardian dear, to whom God's love commits me here,

ever this day be at my side, to light and guard, rule and guide.

Amen.

Reciting it in adulthood, I have made an intriguing discovery. "To light and guard, rule and guide" reveals something I never considered be-fore: my guardian angel is much more than just a protector. The Lord, in his infinite wisdom, has given us these super-intelligent beings to provide guidance and enlightenment, to help us to discern the best choice, not only in difficult decisions, but also in following God's will for our lives.

The ultimate goal for each of us is to be in heaven with God forever. The more I ponder the love of God, the more I realize how illogical it is to think that he would place me on earth without every grace and blessing necessary to fulfill his design for me. He has provided every one of us with a guide, not only in the Holy Spirit, but also in the guardian angels. They are messengers lovingly created and sent by God to every single person to direct us toward heaven.

Trusting Is Not for Wimps

Trusting is not for the faint of heart, as we learn in the passage from Hebrews. It requires endurance. St Paul often speaks in his letters of a marathon of faith, courage, and perseverance — the stick-to-it mind-set that reaps the most significant rewards and blessings. Realizing that God does not make promises lightly is a relatively new revelation for me.

Let me tell you another story about how the Lord used a truck to reassure me of this truth that he keeps the promises he makes. One afternoon as I was driving home from my adoration hour, I pondered a passage in Scripture about God's promise to never abandon us. Having received unsettling news about a friend's health right before arriving at the adoration chapel, I spent most of my holy hour not only worrying about her future, but also thinking about my own mortality and the fragility of life.

"Lord," I thought as I stopped at the light in front of my home, "I can only survive my days separated from you resting in the hope that all you promised in your word is true."

No sooner had I finished my plea for God's reassurance when a truck with the words KEEPING PROMISES emblazoned on its side drove past. The company's name, Old Dominion, piqued my interest, so I came home and looked up the word *dominion*. The words *sovereign*, *like a king*, *lordship*, and *authority* popped off the screen.

If you desire to grow in trust, begin by believing God speaks to you directly, in ways only you and he would recognize ... like, for instance, a giant Mack truck.

Allison's Top Ten Lessons from 1 Thessalonians 5

Lists are my favorite; I love the satisfaction of creating a well-organized list because of the way it pins down all the things swimming around in my head. I also very much enjoy crossing an item off my list. Maybe that is why some of my favorite Scripture verses read like a to-do list. I have also long been a fangirl of top ten lists. 1 Thessalonians 5:14–24 could be described as Saint Paul's top ten list of ways to grow in faith and holiness, not just for ourselves, but also to encourage our sisters in Christ. Although Paul's list contains more than ten items, I have chosen my own top ten. You may make your own list from the passage, but here's mine:

1. **Admonish the idle.** My greatest sin on most days is wasting the time God has given me by being busy but not productive. I am the master of being a busy procrastinator. This can be true of my faith as well: Do I balance the leisure of watching my favorite show or reading a good novel with my prayer time? Am I taking advantage of each moment to grow closer to Jesus?

2. **Cheer the fainthearted.**

3. **Support the weak.**

4. **Be patient with all.** An old friend of mine once advised that one should never pray for patience, because, instead of miraculously gifting you with this virtue, God will instead give you many opportunities to practice it.

5. **Do not return evil for evil.** In our hearts, we may want to even the score or lash out when hurt, but we grow in Christian virtue when we restrain that impulse. It is better to pray for wisdom and temperance in every situation.

6. **Seek what is good [both] for each other and for all.**

7. **Pray without ceasing.** In recent years, I have enjoyed finding different ways to "pray without ceasing." Some of those are pretty unusual, like saying a Hail Mary while filling the coffee maker,

praying for the repose of souls while driving past a cemetery, or praising the Lord for all my blessings while folding laundry or putting away dishes.

8. **In all circumstances give thanks.**

9. **Test everything; retain what is good.** This item calls us to lean on the virtues of prudence and discernment. Spiritual guides in the form of priests, deacons, or godly friends can help us ascertain whether our thoughts or ideas are from God and if they are worthy of our time, talent, or treasure.

10. **Refrain from every kind of evil.**

For me, having concrete ways to grow in faith and to stay connected to God helps me to overcome the anxiety some situations can cause me. Living the tenets of my faith and growing in virtue through doing so also help me to grow in trust of God and to be more at peace as I navigate this life.

Invitation to Share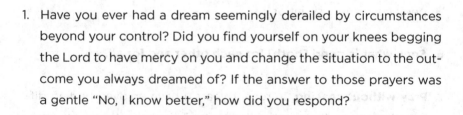

1. Have you ever had a dream seemingly derailed by circumstances beyond your control? Did you find yourself on your knees begging the Lord to have mercy on you and change the situation to the outcome you always dreamed of? If the answer to those prayers was a gentle "No, I know better," how did you respond?

_____

_____

_____

_____

_____

_____

_____

_____

2. How has your faith defined the decisions and choices of your life?

_____

_____

_____

_____

_____

_____

_____

_____

_____

_____

3. How often do you pray to your guardian angel? Do you turn to your guardian angel for counsel and guidance? Can you recount a time when your guardian angel was clearly at work in your life?

_____

_____

_____

_____

_____

_____

_____

_____

_____

_____

_____

_____

_____

_____

_____

Closing Prayer

Jesus, how abundant is your Father's love for us. Your teachings throughout the Gospels help us to recognize his love in all things. You taught us to take full advantage of that love in prayer.

When anxiety is rising within me, how grateful I am that I can seek consolation in you. Many are the avenues to receive your abundant gift of grace. There is no place I can look upon this earth that I will not find you. You mark my coming and my going not with a critical, punishing eye but with opportunities to grow in faith and hope, building a bond of trust between us.

I want to trust you with all my heart. I wish to invite you into those broken places where I tend to allow worry to overcome me. I long to continually feel — without doubt or fear interfering — your love and peace. All things are, indeed, possible with you, Lord. As I continue this journey to trusting you, I will seek an outpouring of grace into my heart and mind.

Lord, I am beginning, even if ever so slightly, to see my old thought processes bloom into new, hopeful, and peaceful dialogues with you. Let this study and my time with it bear great fruit. Amen.

6: Building Trust through the Gift of Hindsight

SEEKING PEACE: A SPIRITUAL JOURNEY

Opening Prayer

Almighty and ever-living God, guide me through this study as I learn how to trust you and accept your desire for me to have no anxiety at all. O Lord, teach my heart to trust in what is to come by remembering what has been — recognizing where you were in the past, especially when I was walking through particularly difficult times.

The beauty of an omnipotent and omnipresent God is no matter where I find myself in this world, you are near. There is nowhere I can go to hide from you. Time does not confine you; I believe you are with me now, in the past, and in the future. There is no moment in my life when you do not accompany me.

Give me the wisdom to accurately discern every memory and recollection so I may see your loving presence and guiding hand. Help me to understand the good brought from each pain, suffering, and disappointment. Strengthen my faith with the memory of each victory, success, and blessing. Sharpen my hindsight so that I may be ever more aware of your work in my life. Amen.

On My Heart

_____

_____

_____

_____

_____

_____

_____

_____

_____

_____

_____

_____

How the Lord Sent Me to World Youth Day to Face My Fear of Death

During one of our Monday night "Bible Babes" meetings, we were talking about overcoming fears. One of the women shared that one of the things she admired most about me was my continuing "yes" to God — despite how frightened I am by most of what he asks! One of the best examples of how God's grace helps me overcome my anxiety is my ability to trust God when he asks me to travel.

The Father Peyton "Godcidence"

One of the places God sent me was Rio de Janeiro for World Youth Day. The inspiration to consider this trip came one day in 2012 as I sat praying at the grave of Venerable Father Patrick Peyton. I have visited his grave many times since being introduced to Father Peyton's ministry by my friend, Christin, in 2007. As I sat listening to the birds and praying with this saint-to-be, I had an unexpected inspiration to attend World Youth Day in Rio de Janeiro the following year — and, more specifically, to travel with the Boston Deaf Apostolate and Father Shawn Carey. Father Shawn is a remarkable priest who, like my daughter, Faith, is deaf. I had been praying for a way to learn how to interpret the Mass for her, and this trip seemed like an answer to that prayer.

My first thought was that even if I could overcome my fear of flying, I lacked any discretionary funds to make the trip happen. The $8,000 cost seemed totally out of reach.

I happened to have with me a biography of Father Peyton written by my former confessor.[8] As I looked at the book, my prayers turned to Father Peyton for help discerning whether to pursue this crazy World Youth Day pilgrimage idea. While I realize I can't seek signs from God like he's a Magic 8-Ball, I longed for a concrete sign from God.

Wondering WWFPD (What would Father Peyton do?), I opened the book randomly, hoping to find any insight the pages might hold. My eyes immediately fell upon three words: Rio de Janeiro!

I quickly emailed the Deaf Apostolate to ask whether I could join their group. It turned out that not only was it possible but Father Shawn had been meaning to ask me to join them! Furthermore, through the fantastic fundraising efforts of the Deaf Apostolate, I was able to attend for free and to bring my seventeen-year-old son for free as well.

Why Did You Bring Me Here to Kill Me?

As this trip seemed anointed by the Lord, I decided to be very brave about traveling ... although, inspired by the story of how Saint Thérèse of Lisieux had gathered stones from the Colosseum on her pilgrimage to Rome, I did bring a rock from Father Peyton's grave in my pocket. There is nothing like a good sacramental to make a Catholic girl feel at ease!

As it turned out, I needed all the help I could get to face the many dangers we encountered during the trip. We were nearly trampled on Copacabana Beach on the opening night, and an eight-year-old pulled a machete on us during our tour of the Favelas (the Rio de Janeiro slums). Then my son's iPod was stolen right from his hotel room, and, to top it off, a very sinister-looking man accosted me in the hallway right outside my room!

The worst night of the trip came when we were nearly crushed by a horde of people trying to exit Copacabana Beach. I turned to Father Peyton for his intercession, and I believe it was he who inspired me to shout out, "Ave Maria!" in a loud, booming voice over and over. Fortunately, even though I was surrounded by people from all over the world, many understood these words, and through this shared language, we could join our prayers together. I could not have been the only person afraid during that perilous effort to leave the beach alive.

Although we did make it out unscathed, I was still shaken when I attended Mass the next morning. We had only been at World Youth Day for one night, and there were many nights we would have to return to that beach. I couldn't understand why the Lord would bring me here to be killed. And that was my prayer: "Why would you bring me here to die?"

The Holy Spirit reminded me that even if that were his plan, I should not fear death. As I sat in this little church praying, the idea of death as a reward and not a punishment popped into my head. Isn't heaven called our "eternal reward"? *Why are you so afraid to meet me,* the Lord asked me, *when you spend your life telling the world how wonderful I am?*

Oh, I want to meet you, Lord, I responded, *I'm just not sure I am currently in any shape to do so — you know, spiritually speaking.* That's what God was calling me to do that day: look at how I was living my life and make the changes necessary to alleviate my fear of death.

If I am called home unexpectedly, I hope to be prepared to meet him. Sure, I'm only human, and there will be a necessity (often) for the sacrament of Reconciliation. But the Lord was calling me to learn more about my faith and, more importantly, to put this knowledge into practice. Faith in action, at least in my experiences, tends to reduce my anxiety significantly.

Faith in Action

I began a devotion for the holy souls in purgatory, praying daily for the dead. I had read in Saint Faustina's diary that the holy souls who benefitted from my prayers would be by my side during my final judgment, so I devised a grand plan: I plotted to have a vast army of saints stand with me before Saint Peter. He would be so distracted by the plethora of souls that he wouldn't notice me slipping quietly around my wall of holy, grateful people, straight into heaven.

In addition to praying the Rosary and adoring the Blessed Sacrament, I also began the Immaculate Heart and Sacred Heart of Jesus devotions. These devotions consist of receiving the Eucharist for five consecutive first Saturdays and nine successive first Fridays. Many promises accompany each devotion, including a happy death. I figured that it wouldn't hurt to have the Blessed Mother's help at my death, in addition to my ginormous posse of holy souls.

To not be afraid can be hard for me sometimes. However, living the tenets of my faith provides me with concrete ways to grow in trust of the Lord. The grace trifecta of prayer, sacrament, and Scripture continues to fuel my resolve to trust.

Every moment we spend speaking to Jesus in prayer, reading the Bible, or participating in a sacrament, particularly at Mass, is an opportunity to encounter Christ. Each encounter with Christ forever changes you as, each time, God molds you more in his image. Drawing closer to him and hiding in the wings of his mighty love, you will find it harder and harder to be afraid.

An Invitation to Ponder

Are you adventurous? Do you let your fears dictate what you will or will not do with your life? Are you willing to trust God enough to follow a life of freedom to go where you feel called, and not miss out on his blessings because you are afraid?

_____

_____

_____

_____

_____

_____

_____

_____

_____

_____

_____

_____

_____

Connecting to Scripture

PRAYER TO THE HOLY SPIRIT BEFORE READING SCRIPTURE

Come, Holy Spirit, come. Fill me with every grace and blessing necessary to understand the message, prepared and waiting for me, in the Scriptures. May my time reading and contemplating the Word of God teach me not only to trust Jesus but also to be open to the peace he longs to give me. Amen.

〽 Psalm 37:3-5 _____

_____

_____

〽 Mark 4:35-41 _____

_____

_____

〽 2 Corinthians 11:21-33 _____

_____

_____

〽 James 1:2-5, 17 _____

_____

_____

〽 1 John 5:1-4, 9-15 _____

_____

_____

Scripture Reflection

In the passage from Mark's Gospel (Mark 4:35–41), we read about a great storm that threatened to capsize the boat that Jesus and the disciples were in. The disciples, worried and afraid, panic; meanwhile, Jesus is calmly resting.

Do you ever feel like Jesus is sleeping while you are on the verge of drowning? I do, and, when I do, I wonder: Why am I tempted to lose hope in Jesus so quickly? Why do the delays in answers to my prayer send me into a tailspin of fear and disbelief? Why do I automatically assume he has abandoned and forgotten me when the storm rages? Don't I have faith? What does unfailing faith look like, and how can I have it one minute and lose it the next?

It's almost as if my faith and my car keys have more in common than I care to admit. They are always in the last place I left them; how quickly I forget where I put them once I get busy with other things.

I think part of my struggle comes from a lack of awe of God. I can become so comfortable in my relationship with God that I forget that he is God — the creator of the universe, the end-all and be-all, the beginning and the end, and my Lord and my savior. We are not collaborators in the field. He is the master, and I am his laborer. I am his servant, in the most beautiful sense of the word. He is my provider, my protector, and, as he should be, my all-in-all. Delight yourself in the Lord, and he will give you the desires of your heart. Delight yourself in his majesty as that is one surefire way to be awed by who he is!

Tossed by the Waves

I often respond like the disciples in the boat, filled with anxiety and fear even though I believe Jesus is right there with me. I don't always have the faith to believe he can provide what I need at that moment. I don't trust that he has my best interest at heart and that he is loving and kind. Nor do I always trust that whatever God allows he will bring good from. I don't want to wait for the good result while I live through the bad situation; I am the kind of woman who skips the sad parts of books. My peace comes in the calm and uneventful. There we see Jesus, our ultimate example of trusting God, content and at rest in the boat amid the storm.

"Do you not yet have faith?" (Mark 4:40) I often pray, "Lord, I do believe, help my unbelief" (Mark 9:24). Where I often fail to trust God is in relying on myself instead of having faith — when I try to rely on my senses, my ideas, and my understanding; or when I try to make God fit into my limited knowledge of who he is instead of seeing him with the eyes of faith. My sight is limited, faulty; even my hindsight is not as reliable as my "faith-sight" can be.

"Blessed are those who have not seen and have believed" (John 20:29). That's who I long to be; I long to be that one blessed by my faith. When the waves begin to churn, like Peter, I quickly succumb to my fears and sink like a rock.

Lord, where are you? Why does it feel like he sometimes hides from us? Why does it sometimes seem that when we cry out, there is no response? If he wants us to believe, wouldn't it make more sense for him to respond to our every beck and call? I mean, surely that would keep me from doubting. I repeatedly ask God to reveal his divinity to me. God has nothing to prove to us, yet he does. He is all we need; he never abandons us, and he is ever-present in our lives. As Scripture reminds us:

> Though the mountains fall away
>> and the hills be shaken,
> My love shall never fall away from you
>> nor my covenant of peace be shaken,
>> says the Lord, who has mercy on you.
>>> (Isaiah 54:10)

And through the prophet Jeremiah, God declares to his people:

> I have loved you with an everlasting love;
>> therefore I have continued my faithfulness to you.
>>> (Jeremiah 31:3, NRSVCE)

Opportunities for Grace

Saint Paul begs the Lord to remove an unspecified thorn from his side (2 Corinthians 12:7). Some scholars believe the thorn represents a chronic affliction. It is left ambiguous so the reader can identify with the message, whatever their suffering. The thorn is an opportunity for grace, not a punishment. How transformative it would be to see our trials as blessings and opportunities to rely on him! Even when he reveals himself, God remains a mystery beyond words: "If you understood him, it would not be God," Saint Augustine said (*Catechism*, 230). Honestly, I don't want a God I can understand, figure out, or fully comprehend. How comforting would it be to follow a God who is no smarter than me? Good grief, no one wants that!

I want the God I have. The One who is Abba, Father; the Alpha and the Omega, who has no beginning and no end. The God who proves his love by sending his only begotten Son to die for my sins. A mysterious triune God, willing to take on my guilt and open the gates of heaven for me. That's the God I want, because, when I cooperate with his abundant grace, he provides for me. I know I can worry less and be at peace more often.

If I spent less time trying to figure out God and more time figuring out who I am in God, the storms would not overcome me. I would see that I am his beloved daughter, provided for and protected; I am a princess of the King of Heaven.

I don't have to *feel* trust; I have come to learn that trust is an act of the will. Our feelings lie, but with the gift of hindsight our reason can acknowledge what he has done for us. There is no hiding from the truth of experiences, especially encounters with God. That's where I can start to build my trust relationship with God.

What's Your Life Verse?

I used to have a friend, who, for her friends' fortieth birthdays, would make a large wooden sign displaying that person's "life verse" — the Scripture that best sums up your relationship with Jesus or the current state of your faith life. You know, your go-to verse.

Over the course of two years, I watched all my friends receive their wooden plaques. I was the last one to reach that milestone, so I had a lot of time to think about what my life verse would be. I finally narrowed it down to Galatians 2:20 (NLT): "It is no longer I who live, but Christ lives in me."

As my birthday approached, I waited for my friend to ask for my verse, but she never did. Unfortunately, our group of friends had begun to encounter some difficulties. Little did I know as we gathered at my favorite Mexican restaurant to celebrate my birthday that we would be embarking on entirely separate lives, never to gather again.

But before the celebration was over, my friend gave me my "life verse" sign. I was perplexed: How could she have made the sign without knowing my verse? I unwrapped the sign to find not Galatians 2:20, but Proverbs 3:5: "Trust in the Lord with all your heart."

What? That's wrong! I tucked the sign under my seat, sadly aware of how far we'd grown apart. How could she have not cared enough to ask what my life verse was?

But here is the funny thing: she had completely nailed it. In the ten years since receiving that gift, I have clung to Proverbs 3:5 far more often than I ever called to mind Galatians 2:20.

Through this broken relationship, the Holy Spirit had given me the promise of his love for me, and a relationship that would never end. Every time I look at that plaque, it reminds me of how trustworthy and faithful God is, and I have lots of examples with which to prove it. We cannot trust one another for everything, and relationships and friendships will end, some with great suffering. But God keeps his promises; God is trustworthy. You can lean on him, even when you don't understand what is happening, and he will always be there to strengthen and guide you. As one of my all-time favorite lines of Scripture says: "We have come to know and to believe in the love God has for us" (1 John 4:16).

Invitation to Share

1. Have any special devotions helped you to grow in faith?

_____

_____

_____

_____

_____

_____

_____

_____

_____

_____

2. What crosses have been particularly hard to carry? Do you believe
   your crosses will always be just the right size and God will give you
   the proper amount of grace to carry them?

_____

_____

_____

_____

_____

_____

_____

_____

_____

_____

_____

_____

_____

_____

_____

3. How do you use your free will to gain and maintain peace in your life?

_____

_____

_____

_____

_____

_____

_____

_____

_____

_____

_____

Closing Prayer

Heavenly Father, thank you for allowing me to see, through all the circumstances of my life, that you are an ever-present God, loving me every minute of every day, never far from me, always willing my good, knocking continually at my heart, ready to shower me with a love that surpasses my understanding the minute I open the door. How can my heart receive such generosity without exploding?

You are always near; how much comfort that brings my burdened soul. My travels, no matter how far from home, never take me out of your watchful eye and loving care. There is truly no place I can hide from you; for that, I am so very grateful.

My mind races with so many memories — cherished moments, deepest despairs, mountaintop experiences. Each molds me into who I am in you, my Lord. Every time I welcome you into my life, you bring blessings beyond measure, and you teach me joy that this world cannot give. I will make it a habit every day to pray for my present, past, and, yes, even my future self. Please cover my life, Father of my heart, in your almighty, merciful grace.

Lord, the waves of my sometimes-stormy life will not disrupt the peace you have put in my heart. I do believe that you will equip me to accomplish all you have called me to. Let this study and my time with it bear great fruit. Amen.

7: Building Trust through Hope

SEEKING PEACE: A SPIRITUAL JOURNEY

Opening Prayer

Almighty and ever-living God, guide me through this study to learn how to trust and accept your desire for me to have no anxiety at all. O Lord, guide my heart in living more fully the grace trifecta of prayer, sacrament, and Scripture. In prayer, I encounter you, face to face and heart to heart. I raise my heart and mind to you, seeking to be filled by your words, love, and abundant grace.

In the sacraments, I experience the outward signs of your abundant grace. All my senses engage in you, the unseen God, through tangible signs I can see, hear, smell, touch, and taste. How great your love must be to provide so many opportunities to meet you physically in Mass, adoration, and Reconciliation, setting my feet back on my path to heaven when sin, doubt, and fear have caused them to wander.

Your Word is truly a light unto my feet. Hearing your voice spoken through your Son, the prophets, and the Apostles closes the gap between heaven and earth, tearing open ever wider the veil that separates us. How gracious and kind you are, my Lord and my God!

Give me the understanding to see these experiences of grace as mere glimpses of *what you have in store for me in the life to come. Help me to hold tight to the hope of heaven. Bless me with the grace to have faith in your magnificent promises even in my darkest hour. Please, Lord, let my life continue to lead toward the eternal reward you have prepared especially for me. (And I hope it includes a tiara.) Amen.*

On My Heart

_____

_____

_____

_____

_____

_____

_____

_____

_____

_____

_____

_____

_____

Transforming Moments

Few things have transformed my life like making time for weekly adoration, frequent reception of the sacrament of Reconciliation, and daily reading of the Scriptures.

I'd never heard of spending time with Jesus in the Eucharist, also known as adoration of the Blessed Sacrament, until a friend's mother introduced it to me in 2007. In *The Gift of Invitation*, I tell the humorous story of how my friend's mother gently encouraged me to sign up for a holy hour. The only available hour, smack dab in the middle of Saturday, was utterly unappealing to me; however, my attempts to elude my friend's mother were unsuccessful, and I ended up agreeing to spend that hour in adoration. Little did I know that her holy persistence would introduce me to a spiritual practice that would transform my life. Furthermore, because that adoration hour coincided with the parish's confession time, this faithful woman also brought me closer to the Lord through the gift of frequent confession.

In His True Presence

Let's begin with how adoration not only changed my faith but provided yet another tool for battling my anxiety. Simply spending time with Jesus regularly grew my faith from a lukewarm Sunday obligation to a holy fire that propelled me to tell the world about Jesus. Adoration transformed my hour in Mass from my get-out-of-hell-free-card obligation (as I was not even sure at first if I even believed in Jesus) to a tangible, powerful relationship with him. This transformation came about, I am sure, from the grace that flows from spending time with Christ in the Eucharist.

This hour of Adoration, the one I struggled to make time for, became the second-most important moment of my entire week (after celebration of the Mass). The graces God bestowed through adoration, especially when I had a million excuses not to go, transformed me emotionally, mentally, and spiritually. When you sacrifice to the Lord the precious commodity of your time, he is never outdone in generosity. Repeatedly, I have seen the time to complete my daily to-do list miraculously multiplied. Not only did I complete all the things I assumed this *interruption* would prevent me from accomplishing, but at the end of the day I miraculously had time for rest as well. Saint Francis de Sales once addressed the old too-busy-to-pray argument in this way: "Every one of us needs half an hour of prayer a day, except when we are busy — then we need an hour."[9]

In those hours of adoration, the Lord enlightened my heart with his love, mercy, and care for me and my loved ones. The more I learned of his unfailing love, the more I began to realize his trustworthiness.

Visits with Grammie

When first presented with the idea of attending adoration for some Jesus time, I thought, "Why do I have to go all the way to the church when Jesus is with me everywhere? I can pray to Jesus from my bedroom, while doing housework, or even while at work. Why do I have to sit with him present in the Eucharist, especially when I am so busy?"

After a few months spending my Saturday afternoons with Jesus in the chapel, I had a "Eureka!" moment. I thought about my grandmother. Sure, I could think about my grandmother, which always brings a smile to my face. I enjoy thinking about her — the funny stories, the yummy food, the gentle hugs. I can go a step further and pick up the phone and call my grandmother. We can have a delightful conversation on the phone, which also brings a blessing to my day.

My favorite memories of my grandmother, however, come from the time I spent in her presence. The stories of her childhood, the sharing of sweet treats, even her gentle correction as I tried to clean her home and never placed the knickknacks quite precisely where they belonged — all of these memories were created because I made the time to be with her physically. The smell of her home, the familiar decor, and the warmth of her face as she smiled upon me are memories and blessings that I will keep with me forever, far more vivid and noteworthy than any conversation I ever had with her.

Considering the blessings that came from these visits to my grandmother helped me realize that when I make time to sit with Jesus, I am blessed beyond measure. I receive grace, encouragement, inspiration, and guidance that I could not get anywhere else but in his presence.

Adoration Never Fails

Some saints have referred to this time of peace and love in the presence of Our Lord as a foretaste of heaven. There are very few things that work to talk me off the anxiety cliff consistently; adoration never fails.

Adoration. Never. Fails. I don't say this lightly as I am very wary of saying anything in this book that would even remotely suggest that if you try a spiritual practice and continue to struggle to trust God, you either don't have enough faith or didn't pray hard enough. That could not be further from the truth of what I hope to share. You are human, and you will have days where returning your heart to a place of peace will come more naturally than other days. It is a journey; it is about the perseverance Saint Paul continually mentions in his letters. This side of heaven, we will never perfect anything, including overcoming our fears and anxieties. That is why I am so grateful to God for allowing us to experience heaven here on earth in adoration. For me it has been the one place that restores my peace, regardless of my state of mind when I entered. Psalm 94:18–19 sums up what adoration does for my anxiety:

> When I thought, "My foot is slipping,"
>   your steadfast love, O Lord, held me up.
> When the cares of my heart are many,
>   your consolations cheer my soul.
>   (NRSVCE)

A Little Help Here

One of the things that can bring me great anxiety is making significant decisions. So many of the most important decisions of my life came while sitting before Jesus in the Eucharist. Our decision to adopt, my husband's decision to join the diaconate, even my decision to close my daycare and enter full-time Catholic ministry. I hold on very tightly to God's promise that if I seek, I will find; if I knock, the door will open; and if I ask, I will receive (Luke 11:9). This includes not only tangible things but also wisdom, hope, and understanding: "But if any of you lacks wisdom, he should ask God who gives to all generously and un-grudgingly, and he will be given it" (James 1:5).

I do not know all things; in fact, I don't know many things, if I'm being honest here. What I do know is that I need God. He knows everything and is eager to share this wisdom with his children. Women seem to be especially adept at taking on the burdens of life all by ourselves. We don't want to bother people, we don't want to be a burden, so instead of seeking help and assistance, we take on the extra responsibility. But the Lord said, "Come to me, all you who labor and are burdened, and I will give you rest" (Matthew 11:28). He wants to help you with your burdens and is not bothered by your prayers.

More Than Just Saying I'm Sorry

Another faith practice that transformed my life is frequent confession. The Sacrament of Reconciliation empowers my heart and my soul to follow God's will for me. Yes, I've got sins I keep repeating, and maybe some that I'm stuck on, but without God's grace I'm never going to overcome them. If I stop going to confession because I know I'm going to sin again, then I would never go to confession. But that's not how it works. When I'm struggling, I am weak; and God reminds us again and again that when we are weak, he is strong. His grace is sufficient in all circumstances, especially in our sins. Saint Paul says that where sin abounds, grace abounds even more (Romans 5:20). The grace that comes from frequent reconciliation helps us to overcome even the smallest sins that we are stuck on. Yes, we will sin again this side of heaven. But the grace that God gives us in the sacrament provides us with the strength to sin less, or, at least, to fall back less often — and, yes, even overcome some of our greatest struggles.

Furthermore, there is something beautiful about hearing the priest speak the words of absolution over me. For many years, I had brought my faults and failings to the Lord, asking for forgiveness. However, I had done it in my room, in the car, or on the beach. But while I knew in my heart that he heard me, I often struggled with whether those sins had, indeed, been forgiven. In the confessional, with Jesus there in the person of the priest, I recognized the gift that the Sacrament of Reconciliation truly is. I heard the words, "Your sins are forgiven." I didn't need to guess; I didn't need to wonder or worry. I was told and could believe. With the words of absolution, the grace was flowing through me. I love when the priest puts his hand on my head as he speaks these words; I can almost tangibly feel the grace moving through my body. I often get goosebumps or even sometimes break down in tears, overwhelmed by God's mercy in my life. (Most priests don't place their hands on the penitent's head during absolution; it's not actually in the Rite of Reconciliation. I just happen to be lucky!)

Speaking my sins to the priest in the person of Christ is humbling, which may be just what my soul needs the most. Just as Adam and Eve's pride got them kicked out of paradise, pride threatens to keep me from entering paradise. It's the root of most, if not all, sin (at least mine!).

Voices in My Head

The third spiritual practice that transformed my life was opening the Bible for the first time and reading God's Word, his love letter to every one of us. This was the answer to my constant prayer: "God, why can't I hear your voice?" I couldn't listen to it because I had no idea how he spoke. Yes, the Mass includes Scripture readings, but I was not aware that they were the Word of God, and I was still lukewarm in the faith and inattentive most weeks. It was reading, physically looking at the words that God has for each of us, that transformed my faith. My relationship with God blossomed when I could distinguish between when I was hearing his voice versus mine. We'll look further at the incredible power of God's Word in the Scripture reflection.

An Invitation to Ponder

Can you name any transformative moments in your life? Do you make room in your life for adoration, the Sacrament of Reconciliation, and daily reading of the Scriptures?

_____

_____

_____

_____

_____

_____

_____

_____

_____

_____

_____

Connecting to Scripture

PRAYER TO THE HOLY SPIRIT BEFORE READING SCRIPTURE

Come, Holy Spirit, come. Fill me with every grace and blessing necessary to understand the message, prepared and waiting for me, in the Scriptures. May my time reading and contemplating the Word of God teach me not only to trust Jesus but also to be open to the peace he longs to give me. Amen.

🖋 Psalm 119:116–117 _____

_____

_____

🖋 2 Maccabees 12:43–46 _____

_____

_____

🖋 Matthew 12:38–40 _____

_____

_____

🖋 2 Corinthians 4:7–18 _____

_____

_____

🖋 2 Timothy 4:18 _____

_____

_____

Scripture Reflection

I am just going to put this out there: My greatest fear is dying. Although some people say they would rather die than speak in public, not me! I would much rather talk in front of a thousand people than die. Sure, the unexpected can happen while you are speaking in public, but, for the most part, I have a good understanding of what is to come next. I also have some general control over the event and its outcome. Death? Well, that's a whole different ball game.

The fear of the unknown triggers my anxiety like nothing else, and the great unknown of death can bring me to my knees. That is an excellent place to be brought to, though, especially if it leads one to prayer. This fear of death has been with me since I was a little girl. From what I can tell, it stems partly from genetics and partly from circumstances. This paralyzing fear has kept me from participating in life's simplest pleasures.

My husband and I have rarely ever traveled beyond where a car can take us. I put off having children until my late twenties for fear of dying in childbirth. The saddest consequence, however, has been the power of my panic attacks to cause me to miss numerous parties, weddings, and family gatherings. I preferred the safety of my home over the dangers of driving to a germ-infested encounter with others. While these fears still plague my thoughts, they don't rule my life. So, what changed?

Scripture Matters

Reading Scripture became part of my daily life. Once I started to learn about God's many remarkable promises of life in the world to come, I was slowly given the grace to overcome my fears and do things despite them. It is not easy; it is very much a daily battle, but one I win more often because I allow God to be bigger than my fears. I want to live and experience this life, and to share the good news of what a life of faith in God can do — not sit secluded in my living room.

This peace is acquired only by seeking the Kingdom of God and moving within the grace found there. Participating in the grace trifecta every day gives me courage. Courage is not the absence of fear but moving forward despite the fear. If you are not afraid, weary, or fighting trepidation, then you do not need courage. Courage is one of the Holy Spirit's gifts — one I receive, open, and use often! After all, a gift left unused is of no use to anyone.

Here is a beautiful plea to hold close to our hearts and ever on our tongues: "Sustain me by your promise that I may live; do not disappoint me in my hope" (Psalm 119:116). Hope in the Lord will never disappoint. Just to be clear: the hope I am talking about is not hope in what I want God to do, but the confidence that comes from surrendering to God's infinite goodness. If I reject God's promises, then whether I intend to or not, I am rejecting God, and I have lost all hope. No wonder it leads to feeling so anxious!

Hope of Heaven

Listen to these words of hope directly from the mouth of Christ: "Rejoice and be glad, for your reward will be great in heaven" (Matthew 5:12).

Holding onto hope is hard. People long before us struggled to believe in the truth of the Gospel. We can only succeed in living this truth when we rely on God to sustain it within us. Ask, believing it will be given to you. When was the last time you reached out to God in prayer and asked for the gift of stronger faith, of a steadfast acceptance of his teaching, and the peace that Jesus promised to leave us?

The Scriptures abound with words of hope, encouragement, and promise of good. Every time I open the pages of the Bible, my heart finds new treasures. The Scriptures are not only God's love letter to us but are also filled with his promises. When read in this light, I arise from my Bible time with an infusion of peace. Who doesn't enjoy being wooed by the one who loves them and comforted by his strength to protect them?

Light and Momentary Afflictions

This verse from Saint Paul conveys my prayer for you; it has brought me much comfort and many consolations over the last ten years:

> Everything indeed is for you, so that the grace bestowed in abundance on more and more people may cause the thanksgiving to overflow for the glory of God. Therefore, we are not discouraged; rather, although our outer self is wasting away, our inner self is being renewed day by day. For this momentary light affliction is producing for us an eternal weight of glory beyond all comparison, as we look not to what is seen but to what is unseen; for what is seen is transitory, but what is unseen is eternal. (2 Corinthians 4:15–18)

The Sign of Jonah

The only sign we need, Jesus tells us, is the sign of Jonah. Jonah's three days in the belly of the fish were a prefiguration of Jesus' resurrection. It's a powerful sign, one that should be enough for me to remain faithful and at peace.

One day, while on the way to the mailbox, I prayed, "Lord, how I'd like a sign that you are here with me in this current struggle."

When I opened the mailbox, it was empty. I laughed out loud at the boldness of the Lord. My mailbox is *never* empty. For the last twenty years, this mail-a-holic has received at least one piece of junk mail every day. The empty box was no accident. It was a clear reminder that the only sign I needed was the sign of Jonah. The birth, passion, death, and resurrection of Jesus Christ, our Lord, is evidence enough that we have nothing to fear. The empty mailbox affirmed that God hears all our prayers — even the flippant ones I mutter on the way to get the mail.

Lessons in Learning to Trust

Over the past seven chapters, we have looked at a great deal of Scripture — each word inspired by the Holy Spirit, each verse a lesson in how to learn to trust God. We catch on to some lessons right away, and we gain confidence in our surrender to God and his will for us. Other lessons require us to rely ever more heavily on grace before we can embrace those lessons as our own. Whether I am in a place of firm belief or wavering hope, I can count on one thing to keep me coming back for more of what God has to offer: "The Lord will rescue me from every evil threat and will bring me safe to his heavenly kingdom. To him be glory forever and ever. Amen" (2 Timothy 4:18).

This comfort that he will always rescue me is precisely what the world cannot give. This reassurance, this hope, exists only in God — Father, Son, and Holy Spirit. This mysterious and marvelous hope is what keeps me on a quest to learn how to trust God fully.

Invitation to Share

1. What do you put your hope in? Is it a struggle to remain steadfast in your hope of heaven? If so, how can you overcome that weakness and remain focused on heaven?

_____

_____

_____

_____

_____

_____

_____

_____

_____

_____

_____

2. How do you imagine heaven? What do you hope it will be like?

_____

_____

_____

_____

_____

_____

_____

_____

3. In what ways can we anchor our hope in God and not allow the unknown of death to produce great anxiety within us?

_____

_____

_____

_____

_____

_____

_____

_____

_____

_____

Closing Prayer

Thank you, Lord, for providing so many incredible lessons in learning to trust you. In our daily needs, sustain us. In our fears, comfort us. May the armor of God always be ready to ward off the arrows seeking to destroy our confidence in Christ.

Remind me often of all the times you pulled me from the pit, set me back upon the rock of your love, and brought light into my darkness. Lavish the gifts of hindsight and hope upon me. In your protective care, nothing can shatter my peace, no matter how fragile it becomes. You will always be my rock and my salvation.

Thank you, Lord, for seven weeks of contemplating, discussing, and learning to trust you. You, who have nothing to prove, humble yourself to demonstrate your love and fidelity to us continually. Who am I, that you, O Lord, are mindful of me? I am a beloved daughter of the Father, you who are the keeper of my heart, mind, body, and soul.

Give me the knowledge and understanding to see these experiences of grace as mere glimpses of what you have in store for me in the life to come. Help me to hold tight to the hope of heaven alongside my magnificent saint posse. Please, Lord, continue to pity my slowness in translating all these lessons into action, but know that I am genuinely trying. May each day bring me closer to trusting you, O Lord, and may it draw me ever closer to that room you have prepared for me in your Father's house (which — have I mentioned? — I really, really do pray includes a tiara).

THANK YOU, LORD!

Notes

[1] If you feel your anxiety requires professional attention, please contact your doctor immediately. Pastoral Solutions Institute (www.catholiccounselors.com) is a reputable and qualified Catholic organization that may also provide you with needed assistance.

[2] Maria Faustina Kowalska, *Divine Mercy in My Soul: The Diary of Saint Maria Faustina Kowalska* (Stockbridge,MA: Marian Press, 2005), 50.

[3] Franciscan Friars of the Immaculate, *Padre Pio: The Wonder Worker* (New Bedford, MA: Ignatius Press, 1999), 117.

[4] *Divine Mercy*, 881.

[5] *Code of Canon Law*, article 110.

[6] *The Didache Bible: with Commentaries Based on the Catechism of the Catholic Church* (San Francisco, CA: Ignatius Press, 2015).

[7] Donald H. Calloway, MIC, *26 Champions of the Rosary: The Essential Guide to the Greatest Heroes of the Rosary* (Stockbridge, MA: Marian Press, 2017).

[8] Richard Gribble, CSC. *American Apostle of the Family Rosary: The Life of Patrick J. Peyton, CSC* (Chestnut Ridge, NY: Crossroad, 2005).

[9] USCCB, "Prayer and Worship," accessed January 30, 2020, www.usccb.org/prayer-and-worship.

The Gift of Invitation:
7 Ways That Jesus Invites You to a Life of Grace
(Stay Connected Journals for Catholic Women)

By Allison Gingras

You're invited to something wonderful — a more abundant life and a closer relationship with God — all you need to do is respond.

In **The Gift of Invitation: 7 Ways Jesus Invites You to a Life of Grace**, you will:

- Discover the seven powerful invitations Jesus extends to you, including the invitation to follow him, forgive from your heart, and know his Father's many gifts

- Explore the Bible to develop a deeper relationship with Jesus

- See how each invitation plays out in your own life

- Reflect on how you can be better prepared to accept Jesus' invitations.

Perfect for individual or group study, the seven chapters includes reflections and scripture, with space for journaling.

Exploring the Catholic Classics:
How Spiritual Reading Can Help You Grow in Wisdom
(Stay Connected Journals for Catholic Women)

By Tiffany Walsh

The Catholic classics are full of wisdom, advice, and inspiration to enrich the lives of modern women, and **Exploring the Catholic Classics** is a great way to access that wisdom and apply it to your life.

In **Exploring the Catholic Classics**, you will:

• Learn about seven inspiring historical and modern works of Catholic literature

• Read selected passages from the writings of St. Thérèse of Lisieux, Pope St. John Paul II, St. Francis de Sales, Thomas á Kempis, and more

• Study these spiritual works in light of the Scriptures

• Reflect on significant spiritual themes and chronicle your own thoughts and experiences

Perfect for individual or group study, the seven chapters includes reflections and scripture, with space for journaling.

Invite the Holy Spirit into Your Life:
Growing in Love, Joy, Peace, Patience, Patience, Kindness, Goodness, Faithfulness, Gentleness, and Self-Control
(Stay Connected Journals for Catholic Women)

By Deanna Bartalini

"The fruit of the Spirit is love, joy, peace, patience, kindness, generosity, faithfulness, gentleness, and self-control," St. Paul wrote to the Galatians. "If we live by the Spirit, let us also be guided by the Spirit" (Galatians 5:22–23, 25). Those words are just as relevant and powerful for you today as they were for the Galatians.

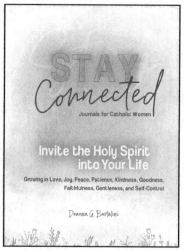

In **Invite the Holy Spirit into Your Life**, you will:

- Learn the life-changing power of the fruits of the Holy Spirit

- Explore each fruit through real-life stories, Scripture, and Church teachings

- Examine how you are cultivating the fruits of the Spirit in your own life

Perfect for individual or group study, the seven chapters includes reflections and scripture, with space for journaling.

Becoming Holy, One Virtue at a Time:
A Guide to Living the Theological and Cardinal Virtues
(Stay Connected Journals for Catholic Women)

By Sara Estabrooks

God calls each of us to become saints. That may seem daunting, but in **Becoming Holy, One Virtue at a Time**, Sara Estabrooks shows you how you can answer this call in your daily life. By drawing on Scripture and the Catechism of the Catholic Church, you will be enabled to seek virtue and pursue sainthood, starting now.

In **Becoming Holy, One Virtue at a Time** you will:

• Grow in understanding of the theological and cardinal virtues;

• Dive into biblical stories that inspire you to become the person God made you to be;

• Reflect on your vocation to holiness in your daily life; and

• Accept God's call to live a life of virtue.